O9-AID-152

LONG WALK
TO FREEDOM

LONG WALK
TO FREEDOM

The autobiography of
Nelson Mandela

Abridged by
Coco Cachalia and Marc Suttner

NOLWAZI

Long Walk to Freedom
Abridged Edition

Original edition first published 1994 by Little, Brown and Co. Ltd.
Copyright © 1994 Nelson Rolihlahla Mandela

Abridgement first published 1996 jointly by Little, Brown and Co. Ltd.
and Nolwazi Educational Publishers, a Macmillan company.
This abridged version first published 1998.
Reprinted 1999
Reprinted 2000 (three times), 2001 (twice), 2002 (three times), 2003, 2004 (twice)
Abridgement copyright © 1996, 1998 Nelson Rolihlahla Mandela,
Macmillan Publishers Ltd and Little, Brown and Co. Ltd.

All rights reserved. No part of this publication may be reproduced, stored in a
retrieval system, or transmitted in any form or by any means, electronic,
photocopying, recording, or otherwise, without the prior written permission
of the copyright holder or in accordance with the provisions of the Copyright
Act, 1978 (as amended). Any person who does any unauthorised act in
relation to this publication may be liable for criminal prosecution and civil
claims for damages.

Typeset in 10$\frac{1}{2}$ on 13pt Carmina
Cover design by Phil Davis
Cover photo by Gisele Wulfson
Language Editor: Gaile Parkin

ISBN 1 919762 87 6

Little, Brown and Co. Ltd.
Brettenham House
Lancaster Place
London WC2E 7EN
UK

Nolwazi Educational Publishers (Pty) Ltd.
P O Box 32718
Braamfontein 2017
Gauteng
South Africa

Acknowledgements

The publishers would like to acknowledge, with thanks,
the following photographic sources:

Anthony Bannister Photo Library p116
Bailey's African Photo Archives p29, p39
Centre for Democratic Communication p149, p150
Mayibuye Centre p10, p25, p35, p37, p46, p59, p77, p80, p90, p107, p138
Times Media Ltd., courtesy MuseuMAfricA ref. no 1/19818 p20

Printed by Intrepid Printers (Pty) Ltd, Pietermaritzburg, KwaZulu-Natal
6987

Contents

Part One

A Country Childhood

M VEZO IS A TINY VILLAGE on the banks of the Mbashe River
in the Transkei. It is surrounded by rolling hills and
fertile valleys. A thousand rivers and streams keep the
countryside green even in winter.

The village is a sleepy and peaceful place where nothing
much has changed for hundreds of years. It was here that I
was born on 18 July 1918.

I was born into the Madiba clan, which is part of the
Thembu tribe. Madiba was a Thembu chief who ruled in the
Transkei many years ago.

My father, Gadla Henry Mphakanyiswa, was a chief and a
member of the Thembu royal family. Although my father could
not read or write, he was a wise man who knew much about
the history of our people. He was a trusted adviser to the king.

When I was born my father gave me the name Rolihlahla,
which means "pulling the branch of a tree". Put more
simply, it means "trouble-maker".

He could not have known what lay ahead of me. But looking back at all the "trouble" I have caused, it was a good name.

My mother, Nosekeni Fanny, was the third of my father's
four wives. Together they had four children, three daughters
and myself.

Altogether, my father had 13 children, four boys and nine
girls. I was the youngest of the boys.

When I was still a baby, my father suffered a great
hardship which was to change our lives forever. He lost his
chieftainship — all because of an ox.

One day, a man complained to the magistrate that one of my father's oxen had strayed on to his land. The magistrate ordered my father to appear before him. But my father, who was a proud man, refused to go to the magistrate. He felt the magistrate did not have the right to summon him — he believed that this was a tribal matter.

My father paid a heavy price for not obeying the magistrate. He not only lost his chieftainship, but he lost his cattle and land as well. We had no choice but to leave our home.

The move away from Mvezo took me to a place where I was to spend some of the happiest years of my life.

* * *

Our new home was in Qunu, a large village near Umtata, where many of our relatives lived. It stands in a narrow, grassy valley surrounded by green hills and clear streams.

Qunu was a village of women and children. The men were forced to leave and work on white-owned farms and mines. They came home once or twice a year to plough the fields. The hoeing, weeding and harvesting were left to the women and children.

From an early age, I spent most of my time playing in the veld with the other boys of the village. I learned how to shoot birds out of the sky with a slingshot, to gather wild honey and fruit, to drink warm milk straight from the cow and to catch fish with sharpened bits of wire.

Our favourite game was a war-game that we called *thinti*. We would stand two sticks in the ground, a hundred feet apart. Each side then had to try and knock the other side's stick down.

After playing with my friends, I would go home for supper. By the fireside, after eating, my mother often told us wonderful stories. These were more than just stories — they carried with them important lessons.

She once told the story of a traveller who met an old woman who could not see because she had cataracts growing over her eyes. The woman asked the traveller for help, but the man turned away. Another traveller came along and once again, the old woman asked for help.

This man was kind — he gently wiped her eyes clean. Suddenly, the old woman turned into a beautiful young woman. They married and became healthy, wealthy and happy.

It is a simple story, but with a strong message: if you are good and kind, you will be rewarded in ways that you can never know.

✿　✿　✿

Both my parents were religious, but in different ways. My father believed in Qamata, the God of his fathers and the great spirit of the Xhosa people. My mother, on the other hand, became a Christian and baptised me into the Methodist Church.

My parents were friendly with two brothers in the village, George and Ben Mbekela. They too were Christians and had a strong belief in the importance of education.

Often, when I was playing or looking after the sheep, the brothers would come and talk to me.

I was just seven years old when George visited my mother and said, "Your son is a clever young fellow. He should go to school."

My mother kept quiet. No one in our family had ever gone to school before. But she told my father what George had said. My father decided to give to his son what he had never had himself — an education.

The schoolhouse was a single room with a tin roof. It stood on the other side of the hill from Qunu.

On my first day of school, my father took a pair of his trousers and cut them at the knee. He told me to put them on and tied a piece of string around the waist. This was the first pair of trousers I ever owned.

Up until then, I had only worn a blanket, like all the other boys in the village. I must have looked very funny in my father's trousers, but I could not have been more proud.

I not only got a new pair of trousers on my first day at school — I got a new name too. In those days, black children were given white names at school because it was more "civilised". My teacher called me Nelson.

Maybe she named me after the great British admiral, Lord Nelson. But that is only a guess.

* * *

One day, when I was nine years old, my father came to visit my mother. I could tell he was not his usual self. He did not talk to me or play with me — instead, he lay in the hut looking pale and thin. He had a terrible cough.

My father's youngest wife, Nodayimani, came to stay with us to help my mother look after him.

A few days later, his coughing got worse. My father called for his pipe. My mother and Nodayimani thought it was a bad idea, but he insisted, and they eventually gave in. They lit his pipe and passed it to him. He smoked for an hour or so, and then with the pipe still lit, he left this world.

Soon afterwards, my mother told me that I would be leaving Qunu. I did not ask why, or where I would be going to.

After packing a few belongings, we set off by foot. We walked for many hours, along dusty roads, up and down hills, through valleys, and across fresh-water streams.

As the sun was beginning to set, we came to a village that lay at the bottom of a shallow valley. In the middle of the village, I saw the biggest and grandest house I had ever seen. We were at the Great Place, Mqhekezweni, where the paramount chief of the Thembu people lived.

My eyes were big, and they grew bigger as the largest and shiniest car I had ever seen drove up. Out of this car, a Ford V8, stepped a short, plump man. He was Jongintaba Dalindyebo, the most powerful man of the Thembu tribe.

When my father died, Jongintaba had offered to be my guardian. He said he would look after me as if I was his own. Jongintaba owed my late father a favour. It was my father who had suggested to the tribe that Jongintaba should become the paramount chief when his father died.

My mother left a few days later, leaving me with these simple words of advice: *"Uqinisufokotho, Kwedini!"* ("Brace yourself, my boy!")

In all honesty, I was not sad when my mother left. Instead, I was filled with excitement. I was in a new world that offered me many new experiences and pleasures.

* * *

At the Great Place I quickly became close to my two new-found cousins, Justice and Nomafu, son and daughter of the Regent, Jongintaba.

I looked up to Justice in every way. He was tall, handsome and a fine sportsman. He was four years older than me and was already at Clarkebury, a boarding school 60 miles away.

The Regent and his wife, who had the unusual name of No-England, brought me up as if I were their own. They called me Tatomkhulu, which means "Grandpa", because they said I was very serious and looked like an old man.

I had a full life at Mqhekezweni. When I was not at school, I was a ploughboy, a wagon-guide, a horse-rider and a bird-hunter.

On Sundays, there was only one thing to do — and that was to go to church. The Regent and his wife were very religious. The only time I ever got a hiding was when I did not attend church one Sunday.

My favourite pastime was listening to the tribal meetings that were held at Mqhekezweni. The Regent was advised by a group of wise men — the *amaphakathi* — who had great knowledge of the history and customs of our people.

These meetings were my earliest lessons in democracy. Every person had a chance to speak in an open and honest way — even if it meant saying things against the Regent. The Regent would keep quiet, and only at the end of the meeting, would he talk. His task was to summarise the discussions and find points of agreement.

At Mqhekezweni I learned about the glorious history of our heroes, such as Sekhukhune, Moshoeshoe, Dingane and Bambatha. The stories of these great African warriors caught my imagination.

The oldest and most wrinkled of the tribal elders was Chief Joyi. He liked to speak about how the Thembu, the Pondo, the Xhosa and the Zulu were all children of one father. The white man had come and divided brother from brother, he said. The white man had seized the land as you might seize another man's horse.

* * *

It is Xhosa custom that a boy only becomes a man after he is circumcised. When I was 16, Justice and I made our way to two grass huts on the banks of the Mbashe River, together with 24 other boys.

The night before the circumcision, women came from nearby villages. Together we sang and danced into the night.

When the sun came up, we bathed in cold water. At midday, dressed in blankets, we stood in two lines, watched from a distance by parents and relatives. When the drums started beating, we sat down with our legs spread out in front of us.

The old *ingcibi* raised his assegai, and with a single blow changed each of us, in turn, from boys to men. As the pain shot through our loins, we cried: *"Ndiyindoda!"* ("I am a man!")

Afterwards, the *amakhankatha* — the guardian — explained to us the rules of entering manhood. We stayed in the huts until our wounds healed.

After the circumcision, there was a ceremony. The main speaker was Chief Meligqili. I have never forgotten the words he spoke that day.

"There sit our sons," he said, "young, healthy and handsome, the flower of the Xhosa tribe, the pride of our nation. We are here to promise them manhood, but it is an empty promise because we Xhosas, and all black South Africans, are a conquered people."

❊   ❊   ❊

The Regent often reminded me that my destiny — like my father's — was to become a counsellor to kings. "It is not for you to spend your life mining the white man's gold, never knowing how to read and write."

So after my circumcision, I was sent to Clarkebury boarding school. The Regent drove me to the school, which was in Engcobo district, in his Ford V8. It was the first time I had ever crossed the Mbashe River.

Before we left, the Regent gave me my first pair of boots. I was so proud that I polished them until they shone brightly.

I learned a lot from the teachers at Clarkebury. They were more educated than the teachers that I had before.

At the school I met students from all over the Transkei, as well as from other places, such as Basotholand and Johannesburg. I also learned much from these students who were more worldly and wiser than I was. But in many ways, when I left Clarkebury, I was still a simple Thembu boy.

❊   ❊   ❊

At the age of 19, I joined Justice at Healdtown, a college in Fort Beaufort, 175 miles from Umtata. It was the biggest college in the country for Africans, with over 1 000 students.

The principal of the college was Dr Arthur Wellington, who liked to remind us that he was from the same family as the famous Duke of Wellington.

Being at Healdtown was like being at a college in England. They tried to turn us into "black Englishmen". We were taught — and we believed — that the best of everything came from England.

The days were long and hard at Healdtown. The first bell rang at six o'clock in the morning. After a breakfast of hot sugar-water and dry bread — I could not afford butter, unlike some of the other students — we had assembly before going off to class.

We had a short break for a lunch of samp, sour milk and beans. Then it was back to class until five o'clock. After exercise time and supper, we studied until nine o'clock. Half an hour later, the lights were switched off.

My best friend at Healdtown was Zacharia Molete. He was Sotho-speaking, and he was my first friend who was not a Xhosa. I remember feeling quite brave at having a friend who was not from the Transkei.

One of my favourite teachers was Frank Lebentlele, who taught zoology. He was popular among the students because he was young and always ready to help us with problems. He was a Sotho and, to our great surprise, he was married to a Xhosa woman. It was not often that you found people marrying out of their tribes.

Another popular teacher was Reverend Mokitimi. One evening he found two prefects having an argument. As he was trying to make peace, headmaster Wellington arrived and demanded to know what was going on.

Rev. Mokitimi told him that everything was under control and that he would report to him the following day. But the headmaster was not happy and again demanded to know what was happening.

Rev. Mokitimi stood his ground and said, "Dr Wellington, I am the house-master, and I have told you that I will report tomorrow, and that is what I will do."

"Very well," said the headmaster. I was amazed. It was the first time I had ever seen a black man stand up to a white man.

But it was not all work and no play at Healdtown. I did some long-distance running and boxing — but being tall and thin, I was much better at running than at boxing. It was only much later in life, when I put on some weight, that my boxing improved.

* * *

At the age of 21, I went on to Fort Hare to continue with my studies. The Regent was very happy that I was accepted at Fort Hare and gave me my first suit to celebrate the occasion. It was double-breasted and grey, and it made me feel on top of the world.

Fort Hare had only 150 students, who were the cream of African society. It was at Fort Hare that I rubbed shoulders with great African scholars like Z K Matthews and D D T Jabavu.

My closest friend at Fort Hare was K D Matanzima. Although he was my nephew, I was younger than him, and according to tribal custom, he was my senior. KD was a third-year student and took me under his wing. He even shared his allowance with me.

It was KD who encouraged me to become a lawyer, even though I had my heart set on becoming an interpreter or a clerk in the Native Affairs department.

The older students did not treat us first-year students very nicely. One of our biggest complaints was that we were not allowed to be on the house committees of our own dormitories.

Fort Hare – here I rubbed shoulders with great African scholars.

One day, the students in my dormitory got together and elected our own house committee. The older students were furious. But we stood our ground and won. This was one of my first battles with authority and it felt good to fight for a just cause.

Besides studying and taking up just causes, I found time for other activities. I played soccer for the first time and continued with my cross-country running.

As a member of the Bible Society, I taught Bible classes to people in the neighbouring villages on Sundays.

One of my fellow students on these trips was a serious young man from Pondoland. His name was Oliver Tambo. I was not very friendly with him at the time, but even then I could see that he would go far in life.

For a simple country boy, Fort Hare was a world filled with new experiences. For the first time I wore pyjamas and brushed my teeth with a toothbrush and toothpaste. Flush toilets and hot showers were a treat for someone who did not have them before.

* * *

During my second year, I was nominated to stand for the Student Representative Council. Before the election, the students met to talk about their problems and grievances. The students were unhappy with the food and wanted the SRC to have more power. They decided to boycott the elections until their demands were met.

When the elections took place, only 25 students voted. Six representatives were elected, of which I was one. The representatives met soon afterwards and decided to resign because we felt we did not have the support of the students.

The principal, Dr Kerr, arranged a second election in the dining-room. He thought that if all the students were present, the election would have greater support among the students.

And so the elections were held again — but once again, only 25 students voted. But this time, the other representatives decided to accept their positions on the SRC.

I did not, because I felt that nothing had changed. I felt that I still could not accept the position.

The principal called me in and asked me to reconsider my decision to resign. He said that if I did not do as he requested, he would be forced to expel me.

I did not sleep that night. Tossing and turning, I wondered if I was doing the right thing. Was I throwing my education and career away? Was the issue really so important?

As I walked into the principal's office the next morning, I was still not sure what to do. "Mr Mandela, have you reached your decision?" he asked. Suddenly, I knew exactly what to do. I told him that I could not serve on the SRC without the support of the students.

Dr Kerr tried to give me a second chance. The summer holidays were coming up and he suggested that I think about my position during the break. If I came back and still refused to sit on the SRC, he would have to expel me, he said.

I was not a happy young man when I left for my summer holidays in Mqhekezweni.

* * *

When I told the Regent about my troubles at Fort Hare, he was furious. He told me that when I returned there I must obey the principal. There was to be no further discussion about the matter.

I decided to let the matter rest for a while, and to enjoy my holiday at Mqhekezweni. Justice, who was now living in Cape Town, was also there. We were happy to be together again.

Then something happened that not only solved my problems at Fort Hare, but changed the direction of my life altogether.

One afternoon, the Regent called for Justice and myself and said, "My children, I fear that I am not much longer for this world, and before I journey to the land of the ancestors, it is my duty to see my sons properly married."

He told us that, according to Thembu custom, he had found women for us to marry. I was to marry the daughter of the priest in the area.

As much as we respected the Regent, Justice and I could not go along with his plans. In many ways, it was because of him that we could not do what he wanted. He had given us an education and allowed us to see a bigger world — a world where people married for love.

Justice and I decided there was only one thing to do. We would run away. Our destination would be Johannesburg.

We secretly planned our escape. We would leave on the morning when the Regent left for a meeting of the Transkei parliament.

We packed the few clothes that we owned into one suitcase. We had no money, but we had an idea of how to get some. We took two of the Regent's best oxen and sold them to a trader in the area. He gave us a good deal, thinking that we had the Regent's blessing.

When we got to the station and asked for tickets to Johannesburg, we were in for a bit of surprise. The station manager had been warned by the Regent about two youngsters who were trying to run away. He refused to sell us tickets.

We made our way to the next station, 50 miles away. From there we caught a train to Queenstown.

In Queenstown we bumped into Chief Mpondombini, the Regent's brother. We told him that we were going to Johannesburg for the Regent and that we needed travel documents. In those days, Africans could not travel around freely.

He took us to the magistrate, whom he knew well. The magistrate was very helpful, but thought it right to telephone the magistrate in Umtata and tell him what he was doing.

As the magistrate in Umtata took the call from Queenstown, he was busy chatting to an important visitor. The visitor was none other than the Regent himself.

When the magistrate from Queenstown told him about us, we heard a familiar voice shouting down the telephone, "Arrest those boys!"

He did not arrest us, but he did not give us travel documents either.

As luck would have it, we met a friend of Justice's, who arranged a lift for us to Johannesburg with an elderly white woman. She agreed to take us, for a fee of 15 pounds. It was nearly all the money that we had.

At ten o'clock that evening, after travelling for many hours, we saw before us a world glittering with lights. Never before had I seen so many cars travelling on the road at one time.

The old woman drove to her daughter's home in the suburbs of Johannesburg. I had never seen such big and wonderful houses. The smallest house was bigger than the Regent's house in Mqhekezweni.

We were sent to the servant's quarters, where we slept on the floor. But we did not mind. Our hearts were filled with excitement. We were in *Egoli*, the City of Gold, and we believed that the whole world was at our feet.

Part Two

Johannesburg

IT DID NOT TAKE US LONG to find out that Johannesburg was not the promised land that we had imagined. The City of Gold was not all glitter and sparkle. It had a dark side.

At dawn on our first day there, we made our way to Crown Mines in search of work, which we needed desperately.

Crown Mines was one of the biggest mines in South Africa. It was an ugly place. A large wire fence surrounded the dusty ground that was scattered with rusty, tin buildings. The noise was deafening. Everywhere I looked I saw black men in dusty overalls looking tired and bent.

We went straight to the chief *induna*, or headman, whose name was Mr Piliso. He was expecting Justice, because the Regent had written to him a few months earlier, asking him to get Justice a job on the mines.

But he looked at me with surprise. Justice pleaded with him to give me a job too. He said there was a letter in the post from the Regent, asking him to help me as well.

The old man believed us. Justice was employed as a clerk and I was taken on as a mine policeman. I started work immediately. I was given a uniform, a new pair of boots, a helmet, a torch, a whistle and a knobkerrie.

It was a simple job. I had to stand guard at the compound entrance under the sign that read: "Beware: Natives Crossing Here."

Justice and I thought we were so clever. We boasted to a friend about how we had run away and tricked our way into jobs. The friend — whom we thought we could trust — went straight to Piliso and told him the truth.

The next day, Piliso called us to his office. He was not his usual friendly self and we knew something was wrong. He showed us a telegram from the Regent. It had five words: "Send boys home at once!"

We had lied to Piliso, and he was angry. He wanted to put us on the first train back to the Transkei. Although we were ashamed of what we had done, we were determined to stay in Johannesburg.

We quickly came up with another plan. We went to see another friend of the Regent's. He was Dr Xuma, a well-known doctor who was also President General of the African National Congress, an organisation that was fighting for the rights of African people.

Once again, we did not tell the whole truth about how and why we came to be in Johannesburg. We asked him to help us to get jobs as clerks on the mines. He sent us to see a Mr Wellbeloved at the Chamber of Mines.

"Well, boys," said Mr Wellbeloved, "I will put you in touch with Mr Piliso at Crown Mines and I will tell him to give you jobs as clerks."

We could not tell him that Piliso had kicked us out of his office a few days before. And so we went back to Piliso with a letter from Mr Wellbeloved, thinking that he would have to obey his white boss and give us back our jobs.

We were wrong. "You boys, you've come back," he screamed when he saw us. "What are you doing here? You'll never be employed on any mine that I run. Get out of my sight!"

Suddenly, we were not feeling so good. There we were in a big, strange city, with no jobs and no place to stay.

*   *   *

Luckily, we had not used up all our contacts in Johannesburg. A cousin, Garlick Mbekeni, who lived in George Goch township, said I could stay at his house for a while.

I told Garlick that my ambition was to become a lawyer. He said that he would take me to see "one of our best people in Johannesburg", an estate agent who knew many lawyers.

A few days later, I found myself in a crowded office in downtown Johannesburg. Behind a cluttered desk sat a man who looked to be in his late twenties. He had a kind and thoughtful face, and was dressed in a double-breasted suit. His name was Walter Sisulu.

Walter, who was then an up-and-coming businessman and community leader, patiently listened to what I had to say. He said that he would ask a lawyer friend if he could give me a job as an articled clerk.

And so, with Walter's help, I got a job at the firm of Witkin, Sidelsky and Eidelman, one of the largest law firms in Johannesburg.

* * *

I was employed at the law firm as a clerk, which meant that I did all sorts of basic tasks — such as filing documents and doing errands. At night, I studied for my BA degree through the University of South Africa.

I shared an office at work with the only other black employee, Gaur Radebe. Gaur, who was ten years older than me, worked as a clerk, interpreter and messenger. I soon discovered that Gaur was a member of both the ANC and the Communist Party.

Gaur was his own man — he was not scared to speak his mind. One day, I entered Mr Sidelsky's office after doing an errand. Gaur turned to him and said, "Look, you sit there like a lord while my chief runs around doing errands for you. One day the situation will be reversed."

Like Walter Sisulu, Gaur was a man who did not have much education — but he seemed to know much more about the world than the educated people I had known at Fort Hare.

Besides Gaur, I made another good friend at the firm. Like me, Nat Bregman was also an articled clerk. He was a bright and thoughtful person, and he was my first white friend. Like Gaur, he too was a member of the Communist Party.

One day, at lunch-time, we were sitting in the office when Nat unwrapped a packet of sandwiches. He took out one sandwich and said, "Nelson, take hold of the other side of the sandwich." I was not sure why he was asking me to do this but, as I was hungry, I agreed. "Now pull," he said. I did so and the sandwich split roughly into two.

As we ate the sandwiches, Nat said, "Nelson, what we have just done is what the Communist Party is all about. We believe in sharing everything that we have."

After work, Nat and I sometimes went out together. He took me to parties where, for the first time, I mixed freely with people of all colours.

* * *

After a brief stay with my cousin Garlick in George Goch, I moved to Alexandra township.

Life in Alexandra was both exciting and frightening. The dirty, dusty roads were filled with half-naked, hungry children. The air was thick with the smoke from coal fires and there were pools of stinking water and sewage everywhere.

It was a poor place and it was a dangerous place — a place that was ruled by the knife and the gun. It was called the "Dark City" — and not just because it had no electricity.

But Alex was also a special place. It was one of the few places where Africans could own property and, more or less, run their own affairs. It was a melting pot where Xhosas, Zulus, Sothos and Shangaans all lived side by side. They were all Alexandrans.

I lived in a shack at the back of a house in Seventh Avenue, which was owned by Mr Xhoma. It had a dirt floor, no heating, no electricity and no running water. But it was a place of my own and I was happy to have it.

Like most other people in Alex, I was poor. The law firm paid me a salary of two pounds per week. Most of this money went towards paying my rent. I still had to find money for food, transport, university fees and, most important of all, candles. I needed candles to study at night because I could not afford a paraffin lamp.

I was always short of money. To save a few pennies, there were many days when I walked the six miles to town in the mornings, and the six miles back again in the evenings.

I often went for days without more than a mouthful of food and without a change of clothing. Mr Sidelsky, who was my height, once gave me an old suit. I wore that same suit every day for almost five years. In the end there were more patches than suit.

My landlord, Mr Xhoma, was not wealthy, but he was very kind to me. Every Sunday he and his wife gave me lunch, which was often my only hot meal of the week. No matter what I was doing or where I was, I made sure that I was always at the Xhomas at lunch-time on Sundays.

In Alex I met up with an old friend of mine from Healdtown. She was Ellen Nkabinde, who was now teaching at one of the schools in the township. Ellen and I fell in love.

It was difficult for us to be alone — there was not much privacy in the crowded township. Often, to be by ourselves, we would walk in the veld and hills surrounding the township.

I loved and respected Ellen, but after a few months, Ellen moved away and we lost touch with one another.

✳ ✳ ✳

At the end of 1941, the Regent came to Johannesburg and sent a message for me to visit him.

When I saw him, I could see that he was no longer angry with me. Not once did he mention my running away from Mqhekezweni.

Instead, he asked me in a fatherly way about my new life and future plans. I was very pleased that at long last we had made peace with each other.

In the winter of 1942, less than six months after his visit, the Regent died. With his passing, a great leader was lost. Through his tolerance and respect for different opinions, he kept his people united. It was a lesson that I would never forget.

* * *

At the end of 1942 I got my BA degree. I had read many books and studied hard — but looking back, I think I learnt just as much from my friend, Gaur Radebe, at the law firm.

It was Gaur who taught me about the long and noble history of the ANC. He lived and breathed the liberation struggle. This was something that I had never seen before.

People rode in trucks during the Alex bus boycotts. The protest lit a fire inside of me.

Gaur took me to ANC meetings, where many issues that affected our people — such as the pass laws, high rents and bus fares — were discussed. I did not speak much at these meetings. I mainly listened.

But after a while, I changed. In August 1943, the people of Alex, under the leadership of the ANC, decided to boycott the buses to protest against an increase in fares. The fare had been increased from four pence to five.

I marched with Gaur and 10 000 others in protest. Nine days later, the bus company dropped the fare increase. A battle had been fought and won.

The march lit a fire inside me. I was no longer an outsider. Slowly but surely, I was becoming part of the struggle for freedom.

✢   ✢   ✢

At this time, I was being pulled in two directions. On the one side, Gaur was leading me into the struggle. On the other side, my boss, Mr Sidelsky, who cared about my wellbeing, tried to warn me about the dangers of getting involved in politics.

"Nelson," he said, "if you go into politics, your career will suffer. You will lose all your clients, you will go bankrupt, you will break up your family, and you will end up in jail. That is what will happen if you go into politics."

Mr Sidelsky was not the only one who tried to give me advice. When I went back to Fort Hare to graduate for my BA, I spent some time with my nephew and friend, K D Matanzima.

KD had already chosen the path of becoming a traditional leader. He urged me to do the same.

"Why do you stay in Johannesburg?" he asked. "You are needed more here."

KD was making a fair point. There were very few Africans with professions in the Transkei, and their skills were badly needed. But I knew in my heart that my duty lay elsewhere. Through my friendship with Gaur and Walter, I saw that my loyalty was to my people as a whole.

* * *

At the beginning of 1943, I enrolled at the University of the Witwatersrand to study for a law degree.

At Wits I met many people who were to share the ups and downs of the liberation struggle with me. During my first term, I met Joe Slovo and his future wife, Ruth First. It was at Wits that I began lifelong friendships with people like Bram Fischer, Harold Wolpe and George Bizos.

I also made good friends with Indian comrades like J N Singh and Ismail Meer. It was at Ismail's flat in Kholvad House in Johannesburg that we spent many an hour talking, studying and dancing until the early hours of the morning.

One day, Ismail, JN and myself were in a rush to get to Kholvad House. We got on to a tram which Africans were not allowed to be on. The conductor told my friends that their "kaffir friend" was not welcome on the tram. He then stopped the tram and called for a policeman to arrest us.

Our arrest and the way the conductor spoke to us came as no surprise to me. It was the kind of thing that happened to our people all the time.

Bram Fischer defended us in court the next day and we were acquitted. It was not the last time that I would be charged in a court of law.

Part Three

Birth of a Freedom Fighter

WALTER SISULU'S HOUSE IN ORLANDO was a warm and welcoming place where you could always get a hot meal and a good political discussion. For me and many others, it was our home from home.

It was at Walter's house, one night in 1943, where I met Anton Lembede, a young leader in the ANC. He had a brilliant mind and a strong personality. I was greatly influenced by his ideas.

Lembede believed that there was a new spirit stirring among the people. Ethnic differences were melting away. Young African men and women were beginning to see themselves, first and foremost, as Africans, rather than as Xhosas, Vendas, Zulus, Sothos, Ndebeles and Tswanas.

He argued that Africa belonged to the Africans who would one day win back what was rightfully theirs. But before this could be done, Africans would have to first regain their pride and self-respect.

Together with Lembede, many young members believed that the ANC had become a tired and soft organisation. We felt that it was time for action. Lionel Majombozi, one of the new young lions, suggested that we form a Youth League as a way of waking up the leadership of the ANC.

The President of the ANC, Dr Xuma, did not think it was wise to start a Youth League. But in 1943, the ANC annual conference in Bloemfontein accepted the idea.

On Easter Sunday in 1944, about 100 young men crowded into the Bantu Men's Social Centre in Johannesburg to launch the ANC Youth League.

Lembede was elected President of the Youth League. Oliver Tambo was the secretary and Walter Sisulu became the treasurer. I was elected on to the Executive Committee.

* * *

At the Sisulu home I met another person who was to become important in my life. It was in their lounge that I met Evelyn Mase, my first wife.

Evelyn, who was Walter's cousin, was a quiet, pretty young woman from Engcobo in the Transkei. At that time, she was training to be a nurse with Walter's wife, Albertina.

I asked Evelyn out very soon after we first met. We quickly fell in love and were married at the Native Commissioner's Court in Johannesburg. We could not afford a traditional wedding or feast.

We had difficulty finding a place to stay. First, we went to live with Evelyn's brother in Orlando East, and later with her sister at City Deep Mines.

In early 1946, Evelyn and I moved into a two-roomed house in Orlando East, and soon after that, to a slightly larger house in Orlando West.

The house was the same as all the other houses in the area. It had a tin roof, a cement floor, a narrow kitchen and a bucket toilet at the back. The bedroom was so small that the double bed took up the whole room. But it was the first true home of my own and I couldn't have felt more proud.

That year our first son, Madiba Thembekile, or just Thembi, was born. He was a happy little boy who, people said, looked more like his mother than his father.

I loved playing with Thembi, bathing him, feeding him and putting him to bed with a story. I have always enjoyed playing with children and talking to them. It is one of the things that makes me feel most at peace.

* * *

The 1946 Passive Resistance Campaign was an eye-opener for the ANC. We began to see the importance of well-planned organisation and militant mass action.

During 1946 two important events took place which helped me to grow politically. The first was the mineworkers' strike.

Seventy thousand members of the African Mine Workers' Union went on strike under the leadership of J B Marks, who was the union's President. The union was asking for a minimum wage of ten shillings a day.

Many of my relatives were mineworkers. During the strike I visited them and spent many hours talking to them. I learned much about the working conditions on the mines.

It was one of the largest strikes in South African history. But the government crushed the strike ruthlessly. Twelve miners were killed and the union was destroyed. Even so, I saw what could be done when people are organised to fight for the same cause. It was my first taste of mass action.

The other important event in that year was the 1946 Passive Resistance Campaign. The Smuts government had passed the Asiatic Land Tenure Act which took away many of the rights of the Indian people. They could no longer own or rent land where they wanted.

The Indian community were angry about the new law which they called the Ghetto Act. They organised a two-year passive resistance campaign, led by Dr Yusuf Dadoo and Dr G M Naicker.

The Indian people organised rallies and marches, and volunteers occupied land in Durban. Two thousand people were arrested and jailed. Dadoo and Naicker were sentenced to six months of hard labour.

The campaign was an eye-opener for us in the ANC. We saw that the freedom struggle was not just about making speeches, holding meetings and passing resolutions.

We began to see the importance of well-planned organisation and militant mass action. Above all, we realised that to be in the struggle you had to be ready to suffer and sacrifice.

*   *   *

In early 1947, after finishing three years of articles at the law firm, I decided to become a full-time student. I wanted to get an LLB so that I could practise as a lawyer.

Giving up my job so that I could study brought great hardship. Evelyn and I were very short of money. I was forced to seek loans from the South African Institute of Race Relations.

At this time our second child, Makaziwe, was born. She was a sickly baby and, right from the beginning, we feared the worst. Evelyn and I took turns staying up with her night after night.

The doctors could not tell us what was wrong with her. When she was just nine months old, Makaziwe passed away. Words cannot describe our pain and grief.

*   *   *

In 1947 I was elected to the Executive Committee of the Transvaal ANC. This was a milestone in my political career. As part of the ANC leadership, I was now bound heart and soul to the movement.

The next year, my life — and the life of the country as a whole — was to change forever. In 1948 the Nationalist Party, led by Dr Daniel Malan, won the whites-only general election.

The Nationalists brought with them a policy called "apartheid" — a cruel system that controlled and oppressed the lives of Africans, coloureds and Indians in every way.

I could not believe that the National Party had won. I was shocked and dismayed. But Oliver Tambo thought differently. "I like this," he said. I could not imagine why. He explained, "Now we will know exactly who our enemies are and where we stand."

Malan wasted no time. He quickly built the foundations of the apartheid system, brick by brick. The pillars were laws such as the Population Registration Act which classified everybody according to race, and the Group Areas Act which forced people of different races to live in separate areas.

The ANC could no longer sit back and watch from the sidelines. The Youth League drafted a Programme of Action calling for strikes, stayaways, passive resistance, protest demonstrations and other forms of mass action. This Programme of Action was adopted by the ANC's Annual Conference in Bloemfontein in 1949.

For the ANC, this was a big break with the past. Up until this time, it had always kept within the law.

Not everybody in the ANC supported this new path. Many of the old ANC leaders were against it, including the organisation's President, Dr Xuma.

At the Conference in Bloemfontein, the ANC elected a new President General. Dr Xuma was replaced by Dr Moroka. Walter Sisulu was elected the new Secretary General and Oliver Tambo was elected on to the National Executive.

* * *

On 1 May 1950, 18 people were killed by the police in a one-day general strike to protest against the pass laws and other apartheid laws.

A few weeks later, the government passed the Suppression of Communism Act. This law not only made it illegal to be a member of the Communist Party — it gave the government very wide powers to deal with any organisation or person who did not agree with its policies.

The ANC — supported by the Indian Congress and African People's Organisation — planned a Day of Protest.

The Day of Protest — which took place on 26 June — was the biggest strike the country had ever seen. Thousands of people stayed home from work. It was a great show of strength.

I was a busy man on the Day of Protest, but I managed to find time to be with Evelyn while she lay in hospital waiting to give birth to our second son, Makgatho Lewanika.

Unfortunately, I was not able to spend much time with my newly-born son — or with the rest of the family. One day Evelyn told me that Thembi, who was then five years old, had asked, "Where does Daddy live?"

At that time, I would return home after he had gone to sleep and leave in the morning before he woke up. I missed family life, but that was the price I was now paying for being so fully involved in the struggle.

✻   ✻   ✻

It was Walter Sisulu who first suggested the idea of a Defiance Campaign. His plan was for volunteers to disobey unjust laws and go to prison.

On 31 May 1952, the ANC, in an alliance with the Indian Congress, announced that it would launch a Campaign for the Defiance of Unjust Laws.

Outside the court after being sentenced to nine months in prison during the Defiance Campaign.

There were to be two stages of defiance. In the first stage, a small number of well-trained volunteers would break specially-chosen laws in some urban areas. They would use toilets, waiting rooms, railway compartments and post-office entrances that were for whites only.

The second stage would be a period of mass defiance which would include strikes all across the country.

The ANC and the Indian Congress created a National Action Committee to run the campaign. A National Volunteer Board was given the task of recruiting and training volunteers. I was appointed volunteer-in-chief and Chairman of both the Action Committee and the Volunteer Board.

On the first day of the Defiance Campaign, more than 250 volunteers around the country were arrested. Together with Yusuf Cachalia of the Indian Congress, I was arrested on the night of the second day as we left a planning meeting. I was kept in jail for two days.

Over the next five months, 8 500 people took part in the campaign. Doctors, factory workers, lawyers, teachers and ministers all defied unjust laws. As they went to jail, they sang, "Hey, Malan! Open the jail doors, we want to enter."

On 30 July 1952, at the height of the Defiance Campaign, I was arrested again. Together with 20 others, I was charged under the Suppression of Communism Act. We were found guilty of "statutory communism" and we were sentenced to nine months' imprisonment with hard labour, suspended for two years.

The Defiance Campaign was a new chapter in our struggle. It had captured the imagination of the people who flocked to join the ANC. The organisation now had over 100 000 members.

The Defiance Campaign left me feeling proud and satisfied. I could now walk upright with the dignity that comes from not giving in to oppression and fear. I had come of age as a freedom fighter.

Part Four

The Struggle is my Life

M<small>Y LIFE DURING THE</small> D<small>EFIANCE</small> C<small>AMPAIGN</small> ran on two separate tracks: my work in the struggle and my work as a lawyer.

In August 1952, I opened my own law office. Business was good — thanks mainly to the help of my secretary, Zubeida Patel. She knew many people in the legal world and brought a lot of business through my door.

At this time, Oliver Tambo was working at a legal firm nearby. I often used to visit him at lunch-time to discuss ANC business. In many ways, Oliver and I were opposites — while I was sometimes heated and emotional, Oliver was cool and collected. I saw that we would make a good team and it was not long before I asked him to join me.

The offices of Mandela and Tambo were situated in Chancellor House, a small building across the road from the magistrate's court in central Johannesburg. It was one of the few places where Africans could rent offices in the city.

We were successful right from the start. Because ours was the only black-owned law firm, people felt that they could come to us with their problems. Every morning, to get to our offices, we had to pass through a crowd of people in the corridors, on the stairs and in our small waiting room.

Day in and day out we heard stories about how our people were suffering in apartheid South Africa.

But it was not only our clients who suffered under apartheid. As black lawyers we were also discriminated against. No matter how many cases we fought and won, we knew that we would never be able to become prosecutors, magistrates or judges.

Magistrates, prosecutors and witnesses often treated us without respect. I remember a case when a magistrate asked to see my lawyer's certificate — something he would never do to a white lawyer.

But when I was in court, I was not bothered by this petty racism. Sometimes being a black man in court was even quite useful.

I remember once defending a domestic worker who was accused of stealing her "madam's" clothes. The "stolen clothes" were on a table in the court. When my turn came to question the "madam", I went over to the table, and with the tip of my pencil, I picked up a pair of panties.

I slowly turned to the witness box and asked, "Madam, are these yours?" "No," she replied quickly, much too embarrassed to admit —especially to a black man — that they were hers. The magistrate dismissed the case.

* * *

At the ANC national conference at the end of 1952, Chief Albert Luthuli took over from Dr Moroka as President General of the ANC. At that same conference — because of my position as President of the Transvaal ANC — I was made one of four deputy presidents. The conference went a step further and made me First Deputy President.

Chief Luthuli was an excellent choice — he was the right man for the job at that time. He was more of an activist than the leaders who came before him, and he was completely committed to the struggle against apartheid.

I could not attend the conference when Chief Luthuli was elected as President. A few days before the conference, I, together with 51 other leaders, was banned from attending any meetings for six months. I was also not allowed to leave Johannesburg.

For me — and for many others — this banning order was the first of many to come. The government was to use bans more and more to silence and sideline people in the struggle.

* * *

Four miles west of Johannesburg, on a rocky hill overlooking the city, stood Sophiatown.

Sophiatown had many names — Softown, Kofifi, Casbah. But names didn't matter. In Sophiatown only living mattered.

Everything happened there. It was the home of jazz. It was the home of politics. And it was the home of gangs — gangs that were big and dangerous, such as the Americans, the Berliners and the Vultures.

Sophiatown — together with Martindale and Newclare — was part of Western Areas townships. It was one of the few places where Africans could own land.

The Government decided to move people out of the townships in the 1950s. It said that the townships were slums — but the real reason was that the government did not want Africans to own property in the cities.

The government divided the people into seven ethnic groups and said that they should move to Meadowlands, 13 miles outside Johannesburg.

These removals were the biggest challenge to face the ANC and its allies since the Defiance Campaign. The ANC held meetings every Sunday morning in Freedom Square in the centre of Sophiatown.

The meetings were lively — people shouted, *"Asihambi!"* ("We are not moving!") They sang, *"Sophiatown likhaya lam asihambi!"* ("Sophiatown is my home; we are not moving!")

At one of these meetings, I made a speech that got me into some trouble. The crowd that evening was feeling angry and wanted action. As usual, policemen with guns — and pencils to take down notes — were everywhere.

I spoke emotionally, saying that the time for passive resistance had ended. I said that violence was the only way to destroy apartheid.

Many comrades on the National Executive agreed with my thoughts — but it was not yet ANC policy. They told me that I was out of order and had put the organisation in danger. I apologised, but in my heart I knew that I was right.

* * *

When my banning order came to an end in September, I took on a case in the little town of Villiers in the Orange Free State. It was an opportunity to breathe in some good country air. In many ways, I was still a country boy at heart.

I left Orlando at three a.m., which has always been my favourite time to set out on a journey. I like to see the coming of dawn, when night turns to day.

The drive to Villiers lifted my spirits, but not for long. When I entered the small court house, I found a group of policemen waiting for me. They were there to serve me with another banning order under the Suppression of Communism Act.

The ban ordered me to resign from the ANC and not to attend any meetings or leave Johannesburg for two years. I had to return home immediately.

Suddenly the fresh air did not feel so good. On the drive back to Johannesburg, the beautiful Free State countryside had lost its charm.

* * *

Throughout 1954 and 1955, we fought an ongoing battle to save Sophiatown. It was a battle that we were to lose.

The people of the township were ready for action. But the leadership of the ANC and its allies decided at the last

Truckloads of families were moved from Sophiatown to Meadowlands.

moment that we were not strong enough to stop the removal.

In the early hours of 9 February 1955, 4 000 police and army troops surrounded Sophiatown. The removal had begun and there was no stopping the government. Truckloads of families were moved from Sophiatown to Meadowlands. Bulldozers crushed the houses to the ground.

The lesson that I learnt from the destruction of Sophiatown was clear: we could no longer fight the iron fist of the government with peaceful methods such as strikes, stayaways, speeches and marches.

A freedom fighter learns, sooner or later, that it is the oppressor who makes the rules of the battle. We realised that we had to fight fire with fire.

* * *

It was Professor Z K Matthews who came up with a brilliant new idea that pushed the liberation struggle in a new direction.

He suggested that the ANC call a national convention. The convention, he said, would be "a Congress of the People, representing all the people of this country, irrespective of race or colour, to draw up a Freedom Charter for the democratic South Africa of the future."

ZK's idea was accepted by the ANC's national conference in early 1955. The ANC immediately got to work with its allies — the Indian Congress, the Coloured People's Organisation and the Congress of Democrats.

Leaders travelled up and down the country, asking people questions like: "If you could make the laws, what would you do?" and "How would you make South Africa a happier place for all the people who live here?"

The people of South Africa answered in their thousands. Suggestions came in from sports clubs, church groups, women's groups, schools and trade unions. They came in on serviettes, on pieces of paper torn out of exercise books and on the backs of our leaflets. The people had spoken.

* * *

The Congress of the People took place in Kliptown, a dusty little village a few miles southwest of Johannesburg, on 25 and 26 June 1955.

More than 3 000 delegates attended the historic meeting. They came by car, by train, by bus, by bicycle, and by foot.

The police were everywhere — but nobody felt any fear. The delegates were there to do an important job and the police and their guns were not going to stop them.

I drove to Kliptown with Walter. We were both still banned, so we looked for a place at the edge of the crowd where we would not be noticed.

Members of the Congress Alliance sat on the platform. The Alliance was made up of the ANC, white comrades from the Congress of Democrats, Indians from the Indian Congress and coloureds from the South African Coloured People's Organisation.

The Congress of the People took place in Kliptown in June 1955.

On the afternoon of the first day, the Freedom Charter was read out aloud to the people in English, Xhosa and Sesotho.

It began with the preamble, or introduction, which started with the historic words: "We, the people of South

Africa, declare for all our country and the world to know ... that South Africa belongs to all who live in it, black and white ... and that no government can justly claim authority unless it is based on the will of the people."

Everything went well until three o'clock the next day, when the police, armed with machine guns, swarmed on to the stage. A policeman grabbed the microphone and announced that no one was to leave the gathering without permission. He said that the delegates were suspected of committing treason.

The police pushed people off the platform and confiscated documents and photographs. They even took away signs that said, "Soup with meat" and "Soup without meat"!

The delegates were then allowed to leave, one by one, after the police had taken down their names.

The police had broken up the Congress of the People. But the Freedom Charter had been written and was there for the world to see.

* * *

The struggle and my work as a lawyer were not my only passions in life. There was one other — and that was boxing.

Although I had boxed a bit when I was a student at Fort Hare, it was only when I came to live in Johannesburg that I took up the sport seriously.

I did not like the violence of boxing. I was more interested in the science of it — how you move your body to protect yourself, how you use a plan to attack and retreat, and how you pace yourself through a fight.

Every evening after work, I would go home and pick up my son, Thembi, and spend a couple of hours in the gym at the community centre.

We all took turns to lead the training sessions in the gym. When it was Thembi's turn to take charge, I always knew I was in for a rough ride.

When he saw me being lazy, he would say in a stern voice, "Mr Mandela, you are wasting our time this evening.

Sparring with Jerry Moloi at his gym in Orlando.

If you cannot keep up, why not go home and sit with the old women?"

Everybody enjoyed these jokes between father and son and it gave me pleasure to see my son so happy and confident.

I never did any fighting at this time, only training. The exercise was a good way of coping with my stress. After an evening's workout, I would wake up the next morning feeling refreshed and ready to take up the struggle again.

Part Five

Treason

JUST AFTER DAWN on 5 December 1956, I heard a loud banging on my front door. I knew immediately that it meant trouble. Only the security police knocked in such a way.

After searching my house from top to bottom, the officer in charge showed me a warrant for my arrest. The words jumped out at me: "*HOOGVERRAAD* — HIGH TREASON".

My children watched as I was led away. Even though I knew that I had committed no crime, it did not feel good to be arrested in front of my children.

I was taken to Marshall Square, a big red-brick prison in Johannesburg. There I met many of my comrades, who had already been arrested. Over the next few hours, more arrived.

Within a week, 156 leaders of the ANC and its allies had been arrested and charged with high treason. The government had made its move.

*　*　*

We were soon transferred to the Johannesburg Prison, or the Fort, as it was commonly known.

When we arrived, we were taken to an outside courtyard and ordered to strip naked. Afterwards, we were put into two large cells with cement floors and one open toilet. There were no beds or chairs, and we slept on mats on the floor.

We stayed in the Fort for two weeks. Even though we lived in terrible conditions, our spirits were high. We listened to political lectures given by the leaders and sang freedom songs.

We were then taken to the Drill Hall for a preparatory examination — this was a hearing to see if the state had enough evidence to put us on trial.

We walked into the courtroom with our thumbs raised in the ANC salute and were greeted by loud cheers from our supporters.

Our first day in court was not very long. The state had forgotten to bring loudspeakers for the courtroom, so we were sent back to the Fort after a few hours.

When we arrived in court the next day, we discovered that the state had built an enormous wire cage for us to sit in. The cage was surrounded by 16 armed guards.

Even our lawyers were not allowed to enter the cage. One of the accused scribbled a message on a piece of paper and stuck it on the side of the cage. It read: "Dangerous. Please do not feed."

Our lawyers — who included Bram Fischer, Issy Maisels and Vernon Berrange — objected to their clients being treated "like wild beasts". They said that if the cage was not taken down, they would walk out of court. The magistrate agreed and ordered that the cage be removed.

Over the next two days, the chief prosecutor read out the charges against us. He said that he would prove that we had plotted to overthrow the government by violence so that we could set up a communist government in South Africa.

On the fourth day, we were released on bail until the trial began. We had to report once a week to a police station, and we were not allowed to attend public meetings.

＊　＊　＊

In 1953, Evelyn gave birth to Makaziwe, whom we named after the daughter we had lost six years before.

But our marriage was in trouble — and had been for some time. Our interests had begun to differ sharply. Evelyn was becoming more and more religious and had become a Jehovah's Witness.

I, in turn, had become more and more devoted to the ANC and the struggle, which upset Evelyn. She had always hoped that I would outgrow my interest in politics and that, some day, I would return to the Transkei to practise as a lawyer.

In those days I was so busy that I was hardly ever at home. I would leave the house very early in the morning and return late at night. Evelyn suspected that I was seeing other women. I told her that I was not but she did not believe me.

When I came out on bail, I found that she had moved out with the children. Our marriage had come to an end.

As in all divorces, the children suffered most. Thembi, who was ten years old at the time, was the most deeply affected. He became quiet and his school work suffered.

After the divorce, he would often wear my clothes, even though they were much too big for him. He missed me very much.

*   *   *

The preparatory examination lasted for much of 1957. At the end of the year, the state suddenly announced that it was dropping charges against 61 of the accused, including Chief Luthuli and Oliver Tambo.

Thirteen months after the preparatory examination had begun, the magistrate decided that there was "sufficient evidence" for putting the remaining 95 of us on trial for high treason.

*   *   *

During a break in the preparatory examination one afternoon, I drove past Baragwanath Hospital, and out of the corner of my eye, I saw a lovely young woman waiting at the bus stop. I was struck by her beauty.

The woman's face stayed in my mind, and for a moment I even considered turning around and driving past her again. But I drove on.

A few weeks later, I walked into Oliver Tambo's office and I could not believe my eyes. Sitting in front of his desk was the very same woman that I had seen at the bus stop. Oliver introduced me to his client. Her name was Nomzamo Winnifred Madikizela.

Winnie, as she was called, came from Bizana in the Transkei and was working as a social worker at Baragwanath Hospital. I am not sure if there is such a thing as love at first sight, but the moment I saw her, I knew that I wanted her to be my wife.

I telephoned Winnie the next day to ask her to help us to raise money for the Treason Trial Defence Fund. It was just an excuse to invite her for lunch.

I took her to an Indian restaurant near my office. Winnie had never eaten hot curry before, and she drank glass after glass of water. This only added to her charm.

After lunch we drove to an open veld near Eldorado Park. I told her of my hopes and dreams, and of the difficulties we were having with the Treason Trial. I told her there and then that I wanted to marry her.

Over the next few months we saw each other whenever we could. She came to visit me at court and at my office. She even came to watch me work out at the gym. Our love for each other blossomed.

We decided to get married at Winnie's home in the Transkei. Since I was banned, I had to apply for permission to leave Johannesburg. I was given six days.

We were married on 14 June 1958. After the church ceremony, many guests attended the reception at the Bizana Town Hall — including a number of security policemen.

At the wedding, Winnie's father, C K Madikizela, spoke of his love for his daughter, my commitment to the struggle and my dangerous career as a politician. He said his daughter was marrying a man who was already married — married to the struggle!

*   *   *

We waited six months after the preparatory hearing for the trial to start. Just before the trial began, the state played another dirty trick: they moved the trial away from Johannesburg to Pretoria.

The trial was now to take place in an old synagogue that had been turned into a court of law.

This was bad news for us. We would be separated from our supporters. Those of us who had jobs in Johannesburg would no longer be able to keep them. This was yet another way in which the state tried to crush our spirit.

We left Johannesburg at six o'clock each morning in a big bus that had hard wooden slats for seats. We returned home late in the evening. All in all, we spent almost five hours on the road each day.

In court, our legal team — led by Issy Maisels and assisted by Bram Fischer, Vernon Berrange and Sydney Kentridge — argued that if the state wanted to prove high treason, it would have to prove that we planned to use violence.

After many days of complicated legal argument, the state suddenly announced that it was dropping the charges against us. We were delighted but we did not celebrate — we knew that the state was planning something.

A month later, the state issued new charges against 30 of us. The others were to be tried later.

After much legal argument, the court finally dismissed the charges against the other accused in the middle of 1959. The case was to continue for the 30 of us who were left.

The state was determined to go on, even though its case against us was weak. The Minister of Justice said, "The trial will be proceeded with, no matter how many millions of pounds it costs. What does it matter how long it takes?"

* * *

Just after midnight on 4 February 1959, I returned home from a meeting to find Winnie alone and in pain. She was in labour.

I rushed her to Baragwanath Hospital. I spent the night at her side, until I had to leave for the trial in Pretoria the following morning.

At the end of the day's hearing I rushed back to find mother and baby doing well. We named our first daughter Zenani which means "what have you brought to the world?"

* * *

Two months later, on 6 April 1959, there was another birth. The Pan-Africanist Congress was born at a meeting attended by a few hundred people at the Orlando Community Hall. Robert Sobukwe was elected President.

The breakaway by some people in the ANC to form the PAC did not come as a surprise. They were influenced by the thinking of people like Anton Lembede and A P Mda. These people believed that Africa was for the Africans and that the struggle was an African struggle.

But the main cause of their breakaway was their objection to the Freedom Charter and to the presence of Indians and whites in the struggle.

The founders of the PAC were well known to me. Robert Sobukwe was an old friend. He had my respect, even though I strongly disagreed with his views. He was a true gentleman and a man who was willing to pay the price for his beliefs.

* * *

The trial against the 30 remaining accused finally began in earnest on 3 August 1959, two years and eight months after our arrests.

During the first two months, the state called 210 witnesses, most of whom were members of the Special Branch of the police. They admitted to hiding in wardrobes and under beds, and pretending to be members of the ANC so that they could get information about the organisation.

The prosecution's case was based, by and large, on a speech made by Robert Resha in 1956. Resha had said, "When you are disciplined and you are told by the organisation not to be violent, you must not be violent. But if you are a true volunteer and you are called upon to be violent, you must be absolutely violent."

The prosecution thought that this proved the case against us. But the defence argued that Resha was not calling for violence. Rather, he had spoken about the importance of discipline in the struggle.

On 21 March 1960, the trial was interrupted by a shattering event.

On 21 March 1960, the police opened fire on an unarmed crowd in Sharpeville and killed 69 people.

The police opened fire on an unarmed crowd outside a police station in the small township of Sharpeville, 35 miles outside Johannesburg. The people were taking part in a demonstration against passes, organised by the PAC.

When the area was cleared and the dust had settled, 69 Africans lay dead. Most of them had been shot in the back as they were running from the police. More than 400 people, including dozens of women and children, had been wounded.

News of the Sharpeville massacre spread across the world. Suddenly, the horror of apartheid was there for all to see. South Africa was never to be the same again.

* * *

After Sharpeville, Walter Sisulu, Duma Nokwe, Joe Slovo and myself held an all-night meeting. We knew that we had to act quickly because the people were very angry. We made plans which we took to Chief Luthuli. He accepted them immediately.

Chief Luthuli publicly burnt his pass in Pretoria on 26 March. I did the same in Orlando, in front of hundreds of people and many members of the press.

Two days later, Chief Luthuli called for a National Day of Mourning and Protest. Several hundred thousand people stayed away from work, and rioting broke out in many areas.

The government declared a State of Emergency. This gave them the power to arrest anybody who opposed their policies and to throw them into jail. And this is exactly what they did.

* * *

On 30 March, I heard that familiar knock on the door at half-past one in the morning. Half a dozen armed security policemen entered my house and, as usual, searched it thoroughly.

They led me away, refusing to tell Winnie where they were taking me. Thirty minutes later, we arrived at Newlands police station, where I found many of my comrades who had also been arrested.

We were put into a tiny single cell with no blankets, food, mats or toilet paper.

At six that evening, we were given sleeping mats and blankets. They were the dirtiest blankets I had ever seen. They were covered with dried blood and vomit, and they were full of lice and cockroaches.

Towards midnight, one by one, we were called out of our cell. I was one of the first. I was taken to the front gate of the prison and released — but not for long.

Before I could move, an officer shouted, "Nelson Mandela, I arrest you under the powers vested in me by the emergency regulations."

We were then taken to Pretoria Local Prison where we were kept in conditions that were as bad as those at the Newlands police station.

A week later, on 8 April 1960, both the ANC and the PAC were banned under the Suppression of Communism Act. Now, just being a member of the ANC was a crime. Members could be punished by a prison sentence of up to ten years.

*　*　*

The Treason Trial continued while we were being kept in prison in Pretoria under the emergency regulations. We would leave for the trial early in the morning and return to the prison in the afternoon.

In April, we decided that our lawyers should withdraw from the case. This would be a good way of protesting against the State of Emergency.

For the next five months, we conducted our own defence. Our plan was simple — to drag out the case until the State of Emergency was lifted and our lawyers could return.

I began giving evidence on 3 August. I looked forward to the chance to speak because I had been silenced by banning orders for three years. I spoke about the ANC's policies and about how we tried by all means to bring about peaceful change.

The State of Emergency was lifted on the last day of August. We would be going home for the first time in five months. Winnie came to Pretoria to fetch me and we had a joyful re-union. It was a good feeling to sleep in my own bed that night.

＊　＊　＊

After the State of Emergency was lifted, the National Executive of the ANC met secretly to discuss the future. We had to find a way to continue with the struggle now that the ANC was banned.

We decided that we would work underground from then on. We also decided that it would be best to shut down the ANC Youth League and the Women's League.

The law office of Mandela and Tambo had already closed its doors. It was not possible to keep the practice going while I was in detention in Pretoria. In any case, Oliver had already left the country.

The leaders of the ANC had been expecting the organisation to be banned, even before the State of Emergency was declared. We had sent Oliver overseas to strengthen the organisation from there.

Oliver's departure turned out to be one of the wisest actions ever taken by the movement. We had no idea at the time how important the external wing of the ANC was to become.

＊　＊　＊

I continued to do whatever legal work I could after I was released from detention. Most of the time I worked from Ahmed Kathrada's flat in Kholvad House.

During this time, I would stay late in Pretoria preparing for the Treason Trial and then rush back to Johannesburg to handle another case.

Winnie was pregnant again. She hoped that I would be at the hospital when she gave birth, but it was not to be.

During the Christmas break in 1960, I learned that Makgatho was ill in the Transkei, where he was studying. I broke my banning orders and went to see him. I drove the whole night, only stopping for petrol.

I decided to bring him back to Johannesburg for medical treatment. I again drove the whole night, and when I got back, I heard that Winnie had already gone into labour. I rushed to the hospital to find that our second daughter, Zindziswa, had already been born.

* * *

The state took a month to do its summing up at the trial. Then it was our turn. Our defence argued that passive resistance and refusing to co-operate were not treason.

In the middle of our argument, the judges asked for a six-day break in the trial. My banning order was due to expire two days later, so the organisation decided to send me to the All-in Conference in Pietermaritzburg.

The aim of the conference was to encourage all South Africans to come together and decide on a new constitution for the country. The conference wanted this to happen at a special national convention.

The National Executive Committee met the day before I left for the conference. They decided that if I was not convicted and sent to jail, I would go underground to organise this national convention. Either way, I would not be returning home.

I knew that going underground would be dangerous and that it would take me away from family and friends. But I knew that it was something I had to do.

When I returned home from the meeting, it was as if Winnie could read my thoughts. She understood what I had to do. I did not tell her how long I would be away and she did not ask.

I could not say goodbye to my oldest son, Thembi, who was at school in the Transkei. I fetched Makgatho and Makaziwe from their mother in Orlando East. We spent some time together, walking in the veld, talking and playing. I said goodbye to them, not knowing when I would see them again.

At home, I kissed Zenani and Zindzi goodbye. They waved to me as I got into the car and began my long drive to Natal.

* * *

I was given a warm welcome by the 1 400 delegates when I walked on to the stage at the conference in Pietermaritzburg.

In my speech, I called for a national convention in which all South Africans would sit down and write a constitution that was fair and just for all. I called for unity and said that victory would only be ours if we spoke with one voice.

A national action council was formed at the conference, and I was made Secretary. Our task was to inform the government of our demand for a national convention.

The conference ended by deciding that if the government did not agree to the call for a national convention, we would call a countrywide three-day stayaway on 29 May.

* * *

"Silence in court!" shouted the orderly to the packed courtroom. It was the morning of 29 March 1961, and after more than four long years, it was time for the verdict in the Treason Trial.

In his deep and even voice, Justice Rumpff gave his judgement. He said it was impossible to believe that the ANC had tried to overthrow the state by violence.

He went on to say that the prosecution had failed to prove that the ANC was a communist organisation or that the Freedom Charter was a communist document.

Justice Rumpff ended by saying, "The accused are accordingly found not guilty and are discharged."

It was a happy moment for the accused and their supporters. But not so for the government. They were embarrassed by the verdict. They would not make the same mistakes again. They would be more ruthless in the future.

Part Six

The Black Pimpernel

I DID NOT RETURN HOME after the Treason Trial. I stayed in hideouts during the day and came out when it was dark. I became a creature of the night.

When I was underground, I did not shave or cut my hair. I dressed as a chauffeur, a chef and a "garden boy". Sometimes I wore blue overalls like a farmworker, and often I wore little round glasses, called Mazzawatees.

Before long there was a warrant out for my arrest. The police looked high and low for me, but I was too slippery for them. I would pop up here and there, much to the anger of the police. But the people loved it.

The newspapers were very interested in my life on the run. There were often front-page stories about me — where I'd been and where I'd been seen. They called me the Black Pimpernel.

I was named after the Scarlet Pimpernel, who was the hero in a story that was set during the French Revolution. The authorities tried hard to capture him — but he always managed to get away.

I myself had a number of narrow escapes. One day, I was driving in Johannesburg and stopped at a traffic light. I looked to my left, and in the car next to me was none other than Colonel Spengler, the chief of the Witwatersrand Security Branch.

I was wearing my blue overalls, a workman's cap and my Mazzawatees. Luckily, Spengler did not look my way. But those few moments at the traffic light seemed to last for ever.

One afternoon I was waiting to be picked up on a street corner. I was wearing a long dust-coat and a cap, pretending to be a chauffeur. Suddenly, I saw an African policeman walking towards me. As I was about to make a run for it, the policeman gave me the ANC thumbs-up salute. We had comrades in unexpected places!

*　*　*

My main task after going underground was to organise the three-day stayaway on 29 May. The government did not sit back and wait for the stayaway to happen — it banned meetings, raided homes and offices, and passed a law that allowed it to detain people without trial.

But the stayaway took place as planned. On the first day, thousands of people did not go to work. It was a good show of strength, but we felt that more people should have taken part.

On the second day, after consulting with my comrades, I decided to call off the stayaway.

That morning, I met some journalists in my hiding-place in a white suburb. I told them I believed that a new day was dawning and that the days of non-violence were coming to an end. The government had violently crushed our peaceful methods of struggle and we now had to think about other ways to win our freedom.

The ANC had debated before about whether or not to use violence. Now Walter and I felt that it was time to discuss it again. We agreed that I would talk about it at the ANC Working Committee meeting in June 1961.

I did not get far at the meeting. Moses Kotane, secretary of the Communist Party and a senior leader of the ANC, said that I had not thought about the use of violence carefully enough. "There is still room for the old methods," he said. "If we embark on the course Mandela is suggesting, innocent people will be massacred by the enemy."

Kotane won the support of the meeting. Even Walter did not back me up. When I asked him why he did not, he laughed and said it would have been as foolish as trying to fight a pride of angry lions.

But he had an idea. "Let me arrange for Moses to come and see you privately," he said, "and you can make your case that way."

Kotane agreed to meet with me and we spent a whole day talking. I told Kotane that he was stuck in the past. People were already preparing for armed struggle and it was the duty of the ANC to guide them. If we did not, I said, the people might move forward without us.

I reminded Kotane of an old African expression, "*Sebatana ha se bokwe ka diatla.*" ("The attacks of the wild beast cannot be stopped with only bare hands.")

In the end, Kotane said to me, "Nelson, I will not promise you anything, but raise the issue again in the committee, and we will see what happens."

When the committee met a week later, I spoke again about turning to violence. This time Kotane was silent. It was decided that I should take my ideas to a National Executive Committee meeting in Durban.

I knew that I would not have an easy time with certain members of the National Executive. It was well known that Chief Luthuli was not in favour of using violence.

At the meeting, I argued again that the people were already turning to violence, whether we liked it or not. It would be better if the ANC could guide and control this violence.

We spent the whole night talking to the Chief, and I think that in his heart he knew that we were right. When someone suggested to the Chief that he was not ready to use violence, he said, "If anyone thinks I am a pacifist, let him try to take my chickens, and he will know how wrong he is."

Eventually the committee agreed with me. We decided to launch a military wing, which would be independent of the ANC, but under the control of the ANC.

We told our Indian comrades of our plans at a meeting

the next night. It was a long and difficult meeting. Some of them were strongly against the use of violence. One of the leaders, J N Singh, put it very simply. "Non-violence has not failed us," he said. "We have failed non-violence."

Finally we reached agreement, and they supported the plan to start a military wing.

This was a historic step for the ANC. We had followed a path of non-violence for 50 years. Now we had chosen a new and dangerous road. We did not know where this road would take us.

* * *

I had never been a soldier, I had never fought a battle, and I had never fired a gun. But now I had been given the task of starting an army.

We called our new army *Umkhonto we Sizwe* — the Spear of the Nation. We formed a High Command which included Walter Sisulu, Joe Slovo, and myself.

* * *

On 26 June 1961, I wrote a letter to the press and explained to the people why I had chosen to go underground. I asked them to join me in the struggle that lay ahead. Part of my letter read as follows:

> I've had to separate myself from my dear wife and children, from my mother and sisters, to live as an outlaw in my own land. I have had to close my business, to abandon my profession and live in poverty, as many of my people are doing ...

> I shall fight the government side by side with you, inch by inch, mile by mile, until victory is won.

* * *

During my first few months underground, I lived for some time with a family in Market Street. Then I shared a flat with a comrade, Wolfie Kodesh, in Berea.

I spent nearly two months in the flat, sleeping on a camp bed. I stayed indoors during the day, with the blinds closed, reading and planning. At night, I left the flat to go to meetings.

I woke up every morning at five o'clock and changed into my running clothes. I would then run on the spot for an hour. This got on Wolfie's nerves, and eventually he had no choice but to join me.

After I left Wolfie's flat, I moved to a doctor's house in Johannesburg. I slept in the servant's quarters at night and worked in the doctor's study during the day. Whenever anyone came to the house, I ran out to the back yard and pretended to be the gardener.

*   *   *

After spending a few weeks hiding on a sugar plantation in Natal, I moved to Liliesleaf Farm in Rivonia. The movement had bought the farm as a hiding-place for those of us who were underground.

I took on a new name at the farm — David Motsamayi — and wore the simple blue overalls of a servant.

During the day, the place was busy with workers, builders and painters who were fixing up the place. I prepared breakfast for them and served them tea in the mornings and afternoons.

The workers would leave at sunset and then I would be alone until the next morning. I left the farm most evenings to attend meetings, and returned late at night.

After a while, Arthur Goldreich, a fellow comrade, moved into the main house. This was safe because the police did not know about his political activities. I moved into the domestic worker's quarters.

Once Arthur and his family had moved in, it was possible for Winnie to visit me. These were happy moments for us — but they were not to last.

* * *

In December 1961, the ANC was invited to attend a conference in Addis Ababa in Ethiopia.

The ANC asked me to lead a delegation to the conference and afterwards to visit as many countries as possible to try and get support for MK, our military wing.

On the day I was to leave, I waited for Walter and Duma Nokwe to bring me my travel documents. I waited and waited — but they did not arrive. They were arrested on the way to meet me.

I had to change my travel arrangements. Ahmed Kathrada organised a lift for me to Lobatse in Botswana. After waiting there for two weeks, I was joined by an ANC comrade, Joe Matthews.

We then flew on together to Kasane in northern Botswana. As we drove into the town, I noticed a lion walking around in the bush. Although I was born in Africa, I was seeing the real Africa for the first time. I felt far from the streets of Johannesburg.

Early the next morning, we flew to Mbeya, a town in southern Tanzania, and then on to Dar es Salaam.

There I met with Julius Nyerere, the first President of Tanzania. I was impressed with Nyerere — he lived in a small house and drove a little car. He was a man of the people.

From there, I flew to Accra in Ghana, where I met up with my old friend and comrade, Oliver Tambo. I had not seen him for nearly two years, and when he met me at the airport, I hardly recognised him. He no longer looked like a lawyer — he looked like a freedom fighter in his military outfit.

The conference in Addis Ababa in December 1961 gave Oliver Tambo and I the chance to tell other African people about the ANC and our struggle.

We then flew on to the conference in Addis Ababa on Ethiopian Airlines. As I was boarding the plane, I noticed that the pilot was black. I panicked — how can a black man fly a plane? A moment later, I felt angry with myself — I had fallen into the apartheid trap of believing that blacks were not as good as whites.

※　※　※

The conference was opened by Haile Selassie, the Emperor of Ethiopia and the great Lion of Judah.

In my speech at the conference, I spoke about the oppression of my people. I explained how all peaceful means of struggle had been closed to us and how we had no choice but to form *Umkhonto we Sizwe*.

The conference was a success. I was surprised to see how little people in Africa knew about the ANC and our struggle. The conference gave us a chance to tell our side of the story and to ask our brothers and sisters in Africa for help.

*　*　*

After the conference, I briefly visited Cairo in Egypt, and then went on to Tunis in Tunisia. There I met President Habib Bourguiba. He offered to train MK soldiers and gave us £5 000 for weapons.

I then went to Rabat in Morocco, which was a gathering place for freedom fighters from all over Africa. It was the headquarters of the Algerian Revolutionary Army and there I learned about the Algerian liberation struggle.

From Morocco, I flew across the desert to Bamako, the capital of Mali, and then on to Guinea. The flight from Mali to Guinea was like catching a bus back home. There were chickens everywhere and women walked up and down the aisle selling peanuts and vegetables. This was people's transport at its best and I enjoyed it very much.

My next stop was Sierra Leone. I visited the parliament there and told a clerk that I was a representative of Chief Albert Luthuli. Before I knew it, the whole parliament queued up to shake my hand. I felt very honoured until I heard one of them mumble, "It is a great honour to shake the hand of Chief Luthuli, winner of the Nobel Peace Prize."

When the Prime Minister came to shake my hand, I tried to explain that I was not the Chief. He would not listen, and so I thought it best to carry on pretending that I was the Chief. I later met the President and told him who I really was. He offered us a lot of money and support.

I then visited Liberia, where I met with President Tubman. From there I went back to Ghana where I met up with Oliver again. Together, we travelled back to Guinea to meet with President Sékou Touré.

Sékou Touré told us that the government and people of Guinea fully supported our struggle. He then went to a book-case and took out two books, which he autographed and gave to Oliver and myself. We could not believe it — we had come all this way just to get books!

A short while later, we heard a knock on our hotel room door. It was a government official with a suitcase in his hand. The suitcase was full of money. It had been worth coming all that way, after all.

Then we met President Léopold Senghor in Dakar. He did not give us the money and support that we asked for. Instead, he gave us passports and paid for our plane fares to our next destination. We were now on our way to London.

* * *

I spent my ten days in London doing ANC business, seeing old friends and seeing the sights. An old friend, Mary Benson, took Oliver and me to see Westminster Abbey, Big Ben and the Houses of Parliament.

When we saw a statue of Jan Smuts near Westminster Abbey, we joked that perhaps there would be a statue of us there one day instead.

* * *

After London, I left for the last leg of my trip — back to Addis Ababa. I had arranged to spend six months there getting military training.

I was taken to a suburb called Kolfe, where I met the man who was to train me. His name was Lieutenant Wondoni Befikadu. He was an experienced soldier who had fought underground against the Italians.

It was tough. We trained from 8 a.m. to 1 p.m., broke for a shower and lunch, and trained again from 2 p.m. to 4 p.m. After that, I was given lectures on military science.

I learned how to use an automatic rifle and a pistol, and how to make small bombs and mines. What I enjoyed most were the "fatigue marches". We were given only bullets and a gun, and told to get to a certain place by a certain time.

The training course was supposed to last for six months, but after only eight weeks I got a telegram from the ANC. They told me it was time to come home. The armed struggle was taking off and the commander of MK was needed.

I flew to Khartoum, and then on to Dar es Salaam. There I met the first group of MK recruits who were on their way to Ethiopia for training. It was the first time that I was ever saluted by my own soldiers. It was a proud moment.

From there I flew back to Kanye in Botswana and drove to Lobatse. There I was met by Cecil Williams, a white theatre director who was a member of MK. Pretending to be his chauffeur, I got behind the wheel and drove us back to Johannesburg that night.

Part Seven

Rivonia

W E ARRIVED BACK at Liliesleaf Farm in Rivonia at dawn. It felt good to be home.

But there was no time to rest. That night the Working Committee held a secret meeting at Liliesleaf so that I could tell them about my travels. The meeting was attended by Walter Sisulu, Moses Kotane, Govan Mbeki, Dan Tloome, J B Marks and Duma Nokwe.

I gave my comrades the good news first. I had received offers of money and training in many of the countries I had visited. The bad news was that many leaders in Africa could not understand the ANC's alliance with whites, Indians and, especially, communists.

I told them that Oliver and I thought that it was time to change the structure of the Congress Alliance. I said that the ANC should be more independent in future. It should be seen as the leader of the Alliance.

This was an important policy decision for the organisation. The Working Committee told me to go to Natal to talk to Chief Luthuli. Everybody agreed that I should go — everybody except Govan Mbeki, who felt that it was too dangerous. His wise words fell on deaf ears.

* * *

I left for Durban the next night with Cecil Williams, once again pretending to be his chauffeur.

I met Indian comrades like I C Meer and Monty Naicker in

Durban, and then I went to Groutville to meet Chief Luthuli. The Chief listened to what I had to say. He said that he did not like the idea of leaders from other countries telling the ANC what to do — but he said that he would think about it.

I met with the MK Regional Command in Durban later that day. This was led by Bruno Mtolo, whom I had never met before. I did not know then that I would meet him again in the future, under very different circumstances.

That evening, some friends in Durban had a party in my honour. The following morning — 5 August 1962 — I met up with Cecil again, and together we began the journey back to Johannesburg.

We made our way through the Natal Midlands, chatting away happily and enjoying the beautiful countryside.

As we passed through the small town of Cedara, I noticed a Ford V8 — filled with white men — rushing past us. I turned around and saw two more cars following closely on our tail.

Suddenly, the men in the Ford signalled for us to stop. I knew, in that instant, that my life on the run was over. A tall, thin man came to the passenger side of the window and introduced himself as Sergeant Vorster of the Pietermaritzburg Police. He had a warrant of arrest in his hand.

The sergeant asked me for my name. "David Motsamayi," I replied. I could see that he did not believe me. "*Ag*, you're Nelson Mandela," he said, "and this is Cecil Williams, and you're under arrest!"

We were taken back to Pietermaritzburg, and locked up in separate cells. I was angry with myself for not having been more careful, but I soon fell asleep from exhaustion. At least I did not have to worry about where I would sleep that night.

*   *   *

I was driven back to Johannesburg the next day and taken to Marshall Square police station. There I was locked up in a cell by myself.

As I lay there thinking about what the future held for me, I heard someone coughing in a nearby cell. I had heard that cough before. I sat up and called out, "Walter?"

"Nelson, is that you?" he answered, and we laughed, not knowing whether to be happy or sad. Walter had been arrested shortly before me. It was not the perfect place for a National Working Committee meeting, but it was a good time to tell Walter about my meeting with Chief Luthuli and how I was arrested.

I appeared in court the next morning and was charged with inciting workers to strike and leaving the country without proper travel documents. Although these "crimes" carried a sentence of up to ten years, I was relieved. It would have been worse if they had found out that I was the commander of MK.

From court, I was taken to the Johannesburg Fort, where Winnie was allowed to visit me a few days later. We spoke about family matters and how she and the children would cope with the difficult times ahead.

When the time came for her to leave, we hugged each other with all the strength in our bodies, as if this was to be our final parting. In a way it was, for we were to be separated for much longer than either of us ever thought.

* * *

The trial was set to begin on Monday 15 October 1962. On the Saturday, I was suddenly told to pack my bags because the trial was being moved from Johannesburg to Pretoria.

Once again, I was to appear in the Old Synagogue, a courtroom which I had got to know so well during the Treason Trial.

I told the court that I would be defending myself and did not need a lawyer. The first thing I did was to ask the magistrate to step down, saying that I did not recognise the court. I asked why I should have to obey laws made by a parliament that I was not allowed to vote for.

I said that it was not possible to receive a fair trial in a courtroom with a white judge, a white prosecutor and white officials.

The magistrate did not step down, and the trial went ahead as planned. The prosecutor called over 100 witnesses to prove that I had left the country illegally and organised the three-day stayaway in May 1961.

When my turn came to call witnesses, I surprised the court. I would be calling no witnesses, I said. I felt there was no point because I was clearly guilty of leaving the country illegally and organising the stayaway.

The prosecutor asked the court to find me guilty on both charges. I would be allowed to address the court the next day before I was sentenced.

* * *

The prosecutor, Mr Bosch, came to talk to me the next morning before court started again. I had known him from my days as a lawyer.

"Mandela," he said, "I did not want to come to court today. For the first time in my career, I despise what I am doing. It hurts me that I should be asking the court to send you to prison."

He shook my hand and said that he hoped that everything would turn out well for me. I thanked him for his kind words and said that I would never forget what he had said.

* * *

My statement from the dock lasted for more than an hour. I explained how I had become the man I was, and why I had done what I had done. When I had finished, the magistrate ordered a ten-minute break.

When we came back the crowded courtroom was silent as he started to read out my sentence: three years in jail for inciting people to strike and two years for leaving the country without a passport — five years in all.

I was allowed to say a quick goodbye to Winnie, who put on a brave face. As I was driven away in the police van, I could still hear the people outside singing, "*Nkosi Sikelel' iAfrika*".

* * *

I was taken straight to Pretoria Prison. My own clothes were taken away from me and I was given a pair of short trousers, a rough khaki shirt, a jacket, socks, sandals and a cloth cap.

I immediately told the authorities that I was not prepared to wear short trousers. Later, I was brought dinner — stiff cold porridge with half a teaspoon of sugar — which I refused to eat.

They gave me a choice. I could wear long trousers and have my own food, if I agreed to be put in a cell by myself, without any contact with other prisoners.

For the next few weeks, I was all alone. I was locked up for 23 hours a day, with one hour for exercise. I had never been in isolation before, and every hour seemed like a year.

I lost track of time. I had nothing to read, nothing to write on or with, and no one to talk to — except the cockroaches.

After a few weeks, I was ready to swallow my pride and trade my long trousers for some company. I was put back with other prisoners after getting a serious warning to behave myself in future.

* * *

One night, towards the end of May, a warder came to my cell and ordered me to pack my things. Ten minutes later, I was taken to the reception area, where I was joined by three other political prisoners — John Gaetsewe, Stephen Tefu and Aaron Molete.

We were told that we were being transferred to another prison. "Where?" asked Tefu. *"Die Eiland,"* was the answer. The Island. There was only one. Robben Island.

* * *

The four of us were chained together and put into a police van that had no windows. We drove all night and arrived at Cape Town docks the following afternoon.

Still chained, we were put on to an old wooden ferry and taken downstairs. The only light and air came from a small window above. This window had another use: the warders enjoyed urinating through it on to us.

It was still light when we were taken up on to the deck. There, before our eyes, was Robben Island. Green and beautiful, it looked more like a holiday resort than a prison.

We were met by a group of white warders shouting, *"Dis die Eiland! Hier gaan julle vrek!"* ("This is the island. Here you will die!")

As we walked towards the prison buildings, the guards shouted for us to run. *"Haak, haak,"* they screamed, as if we were cattle.

I whispered to Tefu that we must set an example — if we gave in now, we would always be at their mercy. Tefu agreed, and together we took the lead and began to walk slowly.

The guards could not believe their eyes. They screamed at us to move faster, but we kept on moving slowly. They ordered us to stop, and one of them shouted: "Look man, we will kill you and nobody will know what has happened to you."

Still we did not go faster, until we reached a stone building. We were taken inside to a large room that was filled with a few inches of water.

We were told to get undressed. As we did so, the guards searched our clothing, and then threw each item, one by one, into the water. Then they told us to get dressed again, which meant putting on wet clothes.

Two officers then entered the room. One of them, a Captain Gericke, angrily asked Aaron Molete why his hair was so long. Aaron was a quiet, gentle fellow and I spoke in his defence. "Now, look here," I said. "The length of our hair is determined by the regulations ..."

Before I could finish, Gericke walked towards me screaming, "Never talk to me that way, boy!" As he was about to hit me, I said, as firmly as I could, "If you so much as lay a hand on me, I will take you to the highest court in the land and when I finish with you, you will be as poor as a church mouse."

He looked at me in amazement. He asked me for my "ticket" and I gave it to him. "Five years! Do you know what it means to serve five years?"

"That is my business," I answered. "I am ready to serve five years but I am not prepared to be bullied. You must act within the law."

Captain Gericke then left the room. He was much quieter than he was when he had entered.

* * *

For the first few days, we were kept locked in our cells and not allowed to go outside. We demanded to be allowed to work, like the other prisoners. This was soon granted.

We worked hard that first day, but on each new day, the warder in charge told us to work harder and harder. Then one day Tefu put down his spade and said, "I will work at my own rate, that is what I am prepared to do, and that is all I can do."

He picked up his spade and began to work again, but at his own speed. Tefu's brave stand — and others like it —

were important to us. Such battles helped us to keep our dignity and self-respect.

* * *

One day, without any warning, a prison official came to my cell and told me to pack my belongings.

Very early the next morning I was taken back to Pretoria, where I was kept in solitary confinement at Pretoria Local Prison.

I heard that many other comrades had also been arrested. I realised that something was wrong.

One morning, as I was walking along the corridor to my cell, I saw the foreman from Liliesleaf Farm. This meant only one thing: the police had discovered Rivonia.

A couple of days later, I was called into the prison office where I found many of my closest comrades — Walter, Govan Mbeki, Ahmed Kathrada, Andrew Mlangeni, Bob Hepple, Raymond Mhlaba, Elias Motsoaledi, Dennis Goldberg, Rusty Bernstein and Jimmy Kantor.

We were all charged with sabotage and told to appear in court the next day. I had served just nine months of my five-year sentence.

* * *

In bits and pieces, I learned what had happened. On the afternoon of 11 July, a dry-cleaner's van had entered the long driveway of Liliesleaf Farm. The van was filled with policemen, who quickly surrounded the property.

They entered the main building and found 12 men sitting at a table, discussing a document. All were arrested, including Arthur Goldreich, who had driven into the farm while the police were there.

The police searched the farm and confiscated hundreds of documents, including "Operation *Mayibuye*", a plan for guerrilla warfare in South Africa.

In one fell swoop the police had captured the whole of the High Command of *Umkhonto we Sizwe*.

*   *   *

A few days later, we were allowed to meet our lawyers, who included Bram Fischer, Vernon Berrange, George Bizos and Arthur Chaskalson.

Bram was worried. In his quiet voice, he told us that we were facing a very serious trial. The state had told him that they would be asking for the death penalty. It was possible that we would be hanged.

*   *   *

On 9 October 1963, we were driven to the Palace of Justice in Pretoria. There were police armed with machine guns everywhere, both inside and outside the court.

As a convicted prisoner, I was forced to wear khaki shorts, which was humiliating. People said I looked unwell. Since my arrest and my long periods of solitary confinement, I had lost 25 pounds.

The trial became known as the Rivonia Trial. The judge was Mr Quartus de Wet, Judge President of the Transvaal. The prosecutor was Dr Percy Yutar, Deputy Attorney General of the Transvaal.

We were charged with sabotage and conspiracy rather than high treason. This was because it was easier for the state to prove sabotage and still get the death penalty.

Bram Fischer stood up and asked the court for more time to prepare our defence. We had only been given the charge sheet that day, while the state had three months to prepare for the case. Justice de Wet gave us a three-week break.

Winnie was not able to attend court that day. She was banned and restricted to Johannesburg and needed police permission to come to Pretoria. She applied and was refused.

Winnie was not the only wife who suffered — Albertina Sisulu and Caroline Motsoaledi had both been detained under the 90-day detention act.

*   *   *

I was allowed to be with the other accused for the next three weeks so that we could prepare our case. It felt good to be in the company of my comrades again.

We were back in court again on 29 October. This time I was allowed to wear a suit, which made me feel a lot better.

Our lawyers attacked the state immediately. Bram Fischer said that the state's case was full of holes. For example, Yutar said I had committed sabotage at a time when I was already in jail! The judge threw the case out of court.

We were free again, but not for long. Even before Justice de Wet left his seat, a Lieutenant Swanepoel tapped each of us on the shoulder and said, "I am arresting you on a charge of sabotage." We were taken back to our cells.

*   *   *

We were back in court in early December. This time we were accused of trying to start a violent revolution and of getting foreign countries to invade South Africa to help us set up a communist government.

The registrar then asked for our pleas. "Accused number one, Nelson Mandela, do you plead guilty or not guilty?"

I stood up and said, "My Lord, it is not I, but the government that should be in the dock. I plead not guilty."

"Accused number two, Walter Sisulu, do you plead guilty or not guilty?"

"The government is responsible for what has happened in this country," replied Walter.

The judge said he was not interested in hearing political speeches. But all the accused ignored him, and each in turn said that he was not guilty and that it was the government that should be on trial.

* * *

Over the next three months, the state produced 173 witnesses and thousands of documents and photographs as evidence.

The state's star witness was Bruno Mtolo or "Mr X", as he was known in court. This was the same Bruno Mtolo whom I had met in Durban just before I was arrested.

Mtolo was a tall, well-built man with an excellent memory. He had been a leader of the Natal region of MK and had visited Rivonia. His evidence — especially about me — made me realise that I was definitely going to be found guilty.

He explained in great detail about the underground activities of MK. Much of what he said was true, but he also told many lies.

When it was our lawyers' turn to question him, we learnt that he had gone to jail three times for theft before he had joined MK. But even so, the judge decided that he was reliable and believable.

The other important part of the state's case was the six-page document "Operation *Mayibuye*". This was our plan for guerrilla warfare and mass armed uprising against the government if sabotage did not work.

* * *

Although we knew there was a good chance that we could be found guilty and sentenced to death, our spirits remained high. We often joked with each other and got up to mischief.

One of our guards was Lieutenant Swanepoel, who was a big, red-faced fellow. He always thought that we were trying to make a fool of him.

One day, while Swanepoel was watching us from the door, Govan Mbeki wrote a note in a secretive way. He then handed me the note, which I read. Nodding seriously, I passed it on to Ahmed Kathrada.

As Kathy took out matches to burn the note, Swanepoel dashed over and grabbed the piece of paper out of his hand. He then left the room to read his prize. A few moments later he rushed in and shouted, "I will get you all for this!" Govan had written in capital letters: "ISN'T SWANEPOEL A FINE-LOOKING CHAP?"

* * *

The state ended its case on 29 February 1964. It was clear that the state had no evidence against James Kantor and very little evidence against Ahmed Kathrada, Rusty Bernstein and Raymond Mhlaba.

It was decided that the remaining six of us would plead guilty to certain charges. There were certain things that we were not prepared to deny — no matter what the cost.

We would not deny that we had turned away from non-violence. We would not deny that we had committed acts of sabotage. But we would deny that we were involved in guerrilla warfare and that we had killed innocent people.

It was decided that I would be the first witness. I would read a statement from the dock, then the others would be questioned under cross-examination. We believed that it was important for us to open our defence with a statement of our beliefs and ideals.

* * *

We were taken to court to begin our defence on Monday 20 April. As I entered the courtroom, I nodded to Winnie and my mother, who had made the long journey from the Transkei to be at my side.

Bram outlined our defence, and then said, "The defence case, My Lord, will commence with a statement from accused number one."

I made my way to the dock and, facing the courtroom, I slowly began to read my statement.

I began by saying that I was a convicted prisoner. I was serving five years for leaving the country without a permit and for inciting people to strike.

From the beginning, I admitted to being one of the people who had helped to form MK. I told the court that whatever I had done, I had done to serve my people and, in a humble way, to contribute to the freedom struggle.

I explained to the court why the ANC had turned to violence. I said that we had no love of violence, but 50 years of non-violent protest had got us nowhere.

I went on to say that although we had turned to violence, we did not plan to kill innocent people. That is why we began with acts of sabotage rather than with guerrilla war or civil war.

But, I told the court, if there was to be guerrilla warfare, I wanted to be able to stand and fight alongside my people. That is why I went for military training in Ethiopia.

I also told the court that the ANC was not itself a communist organisation, although it did work closely with the Communist Party. We had a common goal, which was to bring an end to apartheid.

I spoke about how Africans suffered under apartheid. I said that Africans were given inferior education and inferior health-care and were paid starvation wages.

I said that apartheid had robbed the African people of their dignity. "When anything has to be carried or cleaned," I said, "the white man looks around for an African to do it for him, whether the African is employed by him or not."

All that Africans wanted, I said, was a just share in the country's wealth. Above all, we wanted political rights because without these we would never be free.

At this stage, I stopped reading my speech and turned to face the judge. The courtroom was silent. I did not take my eyes off Justice de Wet, as I spoke my final words from memory:

> During my life-time, I have dedicated myself to this struggle of the African people. I have fought against white domination and I have fought against black domination. I have cherished the ideal of a democratic and free society in which all persons live together in harmony and with equal opportunities. It is an ideal which I hope to live for and to achieve. But if needs be, it is an ideal for which I am prepared to die.

* * *

After my statement from the dock, the other accused took the stand.

Like me, my comrades took full responsibility for what they had done. They stood before the court, filled with pride and dignity, with a strong belief that our cause was noble and just.

After the prosecution and defence had addressed the court, the judge took three weeks to reach a decision.

* * *

On Thursday 11 June we gathered in the Palace of Justice to hear our fate.

Speaking quietly and quickly, the judge gave his judgement. "Accused number one is found guilty on all four counts. Accused number two is found guilty on all four counts."

All the main accused were found guilty on all counts. Ahmed Kathrada was found guilty on one of the four counts. Rusty Bernstein was found not guilty and released.

The judge said he would pass sentence the following morning. We would know then whether we were to live or die.

That night, Walter, Govan and I told our lawyers that we would not appeal against our sentence — even if we were sentenced to death.

Our lawyers were not happy with our decision. But we told them that we wanted to send the message that no sacrifice was too great in the struggle for freedom.

✳   ✳   ✳

The courtroom was full. Amongst the crowd were family, friends and supporters, as well as journalists from all over the world.

My mother (right) with Zindzi (front) waiting for the judgement at the Rivonia Trial. My mother had made the long journey from the Transkei to be at my side.

Before the judge handed down his sentence, two people pleaded on our behalf.

Harold Hanson, a leading advocate, said that the judge should remember that his own people, the Afrikaners, had also struggled violently for their freedom.

The famous author, Alan Paton, was next. He said that the accused had only one choice: "To bow their heads and submit or to resist by force." He asked the court not to punish us too harshly — otherwise the future of South Africa would be bleak.

After they had finished, the judge nodded for us to stand up. His face was pale and he looked nervous. We feared the worst.

He began by saying that he did not believe that we had acted for the good of the people. People who organise a revolution have personal ambitions, he said.

The judge said that he did not have to give us the death sentence. But that was the only mercy he could show us.

And then, in one short sentence, he told us of our fate. "The sentence in the case of all the accused will be one of life imprisonment."

* * *

That night, as I lay on my mat on the floor of my cell in Pretoria Local Prison, my head was swimming with all kinds of thoughts. I thought about the judgement, and about my family who would not see me for a long, long time. I thought about my comrades in the cells nearby, and about how the struggle was going to continue without us.

When the lights went out, the prisoners sang freedom songs, as they did every evening. But that night it was different. The voices were louder and stronger than I had ever heard before. It was as if they were preparing us for the journey that lay ahead.

Part Eight

Robben Island: The Dark Years

AT MIDNIGHT, there was a knock on the door. I was still awake and saw Colonel Aucamp's face through the bars.

"Mandela, you are a lucky man," he said. "We are taking you to a place where you will have your freedom. You will be able to move around; you'll see the ocean and the sky, not just grey walls."

Aucamp was not trying to be funny, but I knew the place he was talking about. It was not a place where I would feel like a free man.

Fifteen minutes later, seven of us — Walter, Raymond, Govan, Kathy, Andrew, Elias and I — were handcuffed and put into the back of a police van.

We were taken to a military airport outside Pretoria, and told to get into an old aeroplane. For the next two hours, we shivered in the belly of the plane, as we made our way to our new home.

* * *

It was a grey, overcast day and the cold winter wind whipped through our thin prison uniforms as we stepped out of the plane.

We were met by guards carrying automatic weapons. They drove us to a stone building, where we were told to get undressed and put on the khaki uniform of Robben Island.

We stayed in the old building for four days before being taken to a stone fortress. There were cells on three of the sides — the fourth side was a 20-foot wall with guards and dogs on top.

We were given three thin blankets, and a straw mat to sleep on. It was so cold that we slept with all our clothes on.

My cell was at the end of the corridor. It was tiny — I could walk from one side to the other in three steps. When I lay down, my head touched the one side and my feet the other.

A white card was stuck on the outside of each cell, with the name and number of each prisoner. Mine read: "N. Mandela 466/64" which meant I was the 466th prisoner to arrive on the island in 1964.

My cell on Robben Island was tiny. When I lay down, my head touched the one side and my feet the other.

I was 46 years old. I was a political prisoner with a life sentence, cramped into a small space that was to be my home for I knew not how long.

* * *

We began to work in the first week, crushing stones with hammers in the courtyard. We sat in four rows, wearing hand-made wire masks to protect our eyes. We were not allowed to talk to each other.

We stopped for lunch at noon. That first week, all we were given was soup, which smelt awful. In the afternoons, we were allowed to do some exercise, under the watchful eyes of the guards.

A huge container for the stones was placed in the courtyard and we were ordered to make it half-full by the end of the week.

The next week, we were told that the container had to be three-quarters full. We worked hard and completed the job.

The week after, we were told to fill the container all the way to the top. Again, we worked hard and managed to fill the container. But we were angry and decided, there and then, that we were not prepared to work in such a way.

The next week we started our first go-slow strike. The guards threatened us, but we ignored them and worked at our own speed.

The struggle had now taken a new form for those of us on the island. We had a new fight on our hands — the struggle to keep our dignity and self-respect.

* * *

Our lives soon settled into a pattern. In prison, each day is like the one before it, and each week is like the one that has just gone by. And so the months and years blend into each other.

Watches and clocks were banned on the island — our only way of knowing the time was by the shouts and whistles of the warders, and by the bells which rang out in the prison. One of the first things I did was to make a calendar on the wall of my cell, so that I could keep track of time.

We quickly realised that the authorities wanted to break our spirit. But their greatest mistake was to keep us together. For together we were able to support and gain strength from each other. We shared whatever we knew and whatever we learned, and through sharing, we became stronger.

From very early on, I knew deep down that I would survive and that my dignity would never be lost. I always knew that some day I would feel the grass under my feet again and walk in the sunshine as a free man.

❧ ❧ ❧

The night warder woke us up at 5.30 every morning by ringing a bell and shouting, *"Word wakker! Staan op!"* ("Wake up! Get up!") After cleaning our cells and rolling up our mats and blankets, we were let out to empty our toilet buckets, which we called "ballies".

We ate breakfast in our cells during those first few months. We helped ourselves to porridge from an old metal drum and drank what was a poor excuse for coffee — ground-up maize which was baked until it was black.

In the middle of breakfast the guards would shout, *"Val in! Val in!"* ("Fall in! Fall in!") This meant that we had to stand outside our cells for inspection.

If the three buttons of our khaki jackets were undone, or if we did not lift our hats as the warders walked past, or if our cells were untidy, they punished us with solitary confinement or with the loss of meals.

We worked in the courtyard until noon, without any breaks. At noon, the bell would ring for lunch and another metal drum of food would be brought in. The African prisoners were given boiled mealies and the Indians and coloureds were given mealie rice. We never got vegetables except for boiled turnips which were so awful that we could not eat them.

After lunch, we worked until four o'clock, when the guards blew whistles for us to line up and be counted. We were then given half an hour to wash up. The bathroom at the end of the corridor had two sea-water showers and a sea-water tap. There were three large metal buckets which were used as bath tubs. There was no hot water.

We were given supper at exactly 4.30. This was mealie-pap again, sometimes with a carrot or a piece of cabbage or beetroot thrown in. Every second day we got a small piece of meat with our porridge. The meat was usually gristle.

Coloureds and Indians were also given a quarter loaf of bread and some margarine. It was thought that Africans did not like bread because it was "European food".

Most times, we got less food than we were allowed. This was because the cooks — who were all prisoners too — kept the best food for themselves and their friends.

At eight o'clock the night warder would lock himself in with us and order us to go to sleep. There was no such thing as "lights out" — because the lights in the cells were kept on day and night.

Before going to sleep, we would try to talk to each other without the warder hearing. If he did hear us, he would shout at us to keep quiet. Later on, we learnt a trick — we would sprinkle sand along the corridor so that we could hear the warder's footsteps before he came.

* * *

In jail, every man was classified as an A,B,C or D prisoner. A was the highest category with the most privileges, and D the lowest, with the fewest privileges. All political prisoners were classified D when they first arrived.

Every six months there was a hearing to decide whether a prisoner would go up a grade. The fastest way for a prisoner to get a higher classification was to behave and not to complain. I refused to go along with this and the warders would often say, "Ag, Mandela, you are a trouble-maker, you will be in D group for the rest of your life."

As a D-group prisoner I was allowed to have one visitor and write and receive one letter every six months. I found this one of the heaviest burdens of prison life.

Often, out of spite, the authorities would not pass on that one all-important letter. They would say: "Mandela, we have received a letter for you, but we cannot give it to you." They would not explain why or who the letter was from.

During the first few months, I received one letter from Winnie, most of which had been blotted out with ink by the authorities. We soon learned that we could wash away the ink and read what was underneath. Later on, they got wise and used razors to cut pieces out of our letters.

The letters we wrote were treated in the same way; they were often cut up as much as those we received.

*　*　*

After I had been on the island for less than three months, I was told that I would be getting a visitor the next day. I hoped with all my heart that it would be Winnie.

The prison authorities made it difficult for the families of prisoners to visit. They would contact a prisoner's wife and say, "You have permission to visit your husband tomorrow."

Many of the prisoners' families lived far from the Cape and they could not afford the trip to Robben Island. There were men on the island who did not see their wives for many years at a time. I knew of men who went for ten years or more without a single visit.

Political prisoners were only allowed "non-contact" visits. This meant that they had to talk to their loved ones through thick glass — in English or Afrikaans only. The visitors' room was tiny and it had no windows.

I was called to the visitors' room in the late morning and waited nervously. Suddenly, Winnie's lovely face filled the glass on the other side of the window.

I told Winnie that I was fine and asked about the children and the rest of the family. We had hardly spoken when the warder behind me shouted, "Time up! Time up!"

Over the next days, weeks and months, I would think about the visit again and again. I knew that I would not be able to see my wife for at least another six months. I did not know then that Winnie would not be allowed to visit me for another two years.

* * *

One day in January, as we were lining up to be counted before starting work in the courtyard, we were told to go outside and get into a covered truck. It was the first time that we had ever left the compound.

A few minutes later, the truck stopped at a place that I had first seen when I was on the island in 1962: the lime quarry.

The lime quarry was a big hole that was cut into the hillside. The light that shone off the bright white rock was blinding.

The Commanding Officer, Colonel Wessels, came to the quarry and told us that we would be working there for six months. He promised that we would get light work after that. He was a bit off with his timing: we remained at the quarry for the next 13 years.

We were given picks and shovels, and a quick lesson on how to mine lime. It is not a simple task. The lime is buried in layers of rock which have to be broken out with a pick and then removed with a shovel. This was much harder than working in the courtyard.

Making us work on the lime quarry was their way of trying to break our spirit. But it had the opposite effect.

I loved being outside in nature, being able to see grass and trees, to watch the birds fly overhead, and to feel the wind blowing in from the sea. It felt good to use all my muscles, with the sun on my back, and there was a simple pleasure in making piles of lime.

By the end of the day, our faces and bodies were covered in white dust, which made us look like ghosts. When we returned to our cells, we scrubbed ourselves with cold water, but the dust never seemed to wash away completely.

* * *

Working on the quarry may have been good for our spirits, but it was bad for our eyes. The sun's rays reflected off the lime, and the brightness and the dust made it difficult for us to see.

After our first few days at the quarry, we asked for sunglasses. These were refused. We were not surprised because, at this time, we were not even allowed reading glasses.

It took three years before we were allowed to wear sunglasses. Even then, we had to pay for the glasses ourselves.

* * *

One day in the summer of 1965, we discovered some fat in our porridge at breakfast. At supper-time there were pieces of meat with our pap. The next day some of us got new shirts. Even the guards at the quarry were nice to us. We were suspicious, because you never get something for nothing in prison.

We were told a day later that the International Red Cross would be visiting. This was an important visit because the Red Cross was a powerful organisation. The prison authorities feared them.

On the day of the visit, I was called to meet the Red Cross representative, a Mr Senn. I complained about our clothing and told him how we hated wearing short trousers. I also mentioned that we were not given socks or underwear, which we needed. I also complained about the food, lack of exercise, hard labour and the behaviour of the warders.

Not long after the visit from Mr Senn, we were given long trousers. In those early years, the International Red Cross was the only organisation that listened to our complaints and tried to help us.

Later, the Red Cross helped us by giving money to our wives and relatives. This made it possible for many of them to visit us on the island. Without this help, they would not have been able to do so.

* * *

A few months after we arrived on Robben Island, the authorities said that we could apply for permission to study.

Some of the men registered for university courses, while others worked towards finishing their high school education. Within months, nearly all of us were studying for one qualification or another. At night, our cell block seemed more like a study hall than a prison.

But the study privileges came with a string of conditions. We were not allowed to study subjects like politics or military history.

For a long time, prisoners were only permitted to get money to study from their families. This made it very difficult for those who came from poor families. We were not even allowed to lend our books to each other, which would have made it much easier for the poorer prisoners.

* * *

One of the biggest hardships for us on the island was being cut off from the outside world. We were starved of news.

Over the years, we thought of all kinds of ways to get our hands on newspapers. At the quarry, we would pick up the pieces of newspaper that the warders used to wrap their sandwiches in. We hid these under our shirts to read later.

The easiest way of getting newspapers was by bribing the warders. They were often short of money and we used this to our advantage.

When we did get hold of a newspaper, it was much too dangerous to pass it around. Instead, one person, usually Kathy, would read through the paper and cut out articles. These were then secretly given to others. They would make summaries of the stories and then pass them to the rest of us.

One day, after returning from exercise in the courtyard, I noticed that a warder had left a newspaper on a bench at the end of the corridor.

I quickly left my cell, walked to the end of the corridor, looked in both directions, and hid the newspaper inside my shirt.

Usually, I would have hidden the newspaper somewhere in my cell and taken it out only after bedtime. But, like a child who eats his pudding before his main course, I opened the paper immediately because I was so hungry for news.

I was so busy reading that I did not even hear the footsteps of the warder, and before I knew it, he was standing in front of me. I did not even have time to slide the paper under my mat.

"Mandela," the warder said, "we are charging you for possession of contraband and you will pay for this."

A magistrate was brought from Cape Town within two days. He sentenced me to three days in isolation.

In solitary confinement you had no company and got no exercise or food. You were given only rice water three times a day. (Rice water is water in which rice has been boiled.)

This was the first time that I was put into isolation, but not the last. In fact, in those early years, it became quite a habit for me.

❊   ❊   ❊

Another way of getting news was from other prisoners on the island. Our comrades in the general section had more information about the ANC and about our friends and families, because there were many more prisoners coming and going there.

We organised a secret committee whose job was to find ways of making contact with the other prisoners.

One of the first tricks for doing this was invented by Kathy and Mac Maharaj. They collected empty matchboxes and made false bottoms in them. Secret messages could be hidden inside these false bottoms. On the way to the quarry, they dropped the matchboxes at certain points where they knew the general prisoners would pass. The general prisoners picked up the matchboxes, read the messages, and replied in the same way.

We also placed messages at the bottom of food drums. These drums were then taken back to the kitchen by the general section prisoners who worked there.

Another way was to place messages wrapped in plastic in the toilet bowls in the isolation section. We encouraged our comrades from the general section to be charged and be put in isolation so that they could collect the messages.

We also discovered clever ways of writing notes which the authorities could not read. One way was to write notes with milk. The milk dried almost immediately so that the paper looked blank. But when we sprayed the paper with the disinfectant that we used for cleaning our cells, the writing became visible again.

One of the most popular methods of smuggling out messages was to write them on pieces of toilet paper, using a secret code. This worked well most of the time.

But the best way of all was to get sent to the prison hospital. There you met up with prisoners from all the sections. Sometimes prisoners from different sections even shared the same ward and were able to speak to one another freely.

We made contact with the outside world in two ways: we sent messages with prisoners who were leaving the island and with visitors, especially lawyers, who were not searched.

*   *   *

In July 1966, we learnt that the men in the general section had started a hunger-strike. This news came to us in a note hidden in our food drum. The note was not very clear and we were not exactly sure why they had started the strike or when. But we decided to support the strike to show our solidarity with the other prisoners.

During the first day of our hunger-strike we were served with our normal food and we refused to eat it. On the second day, we noticed that our portions were larger and there were more vegetables. On the third day, juicy pieces of meat were served with supper. By the fourth day, the porridge was served with big chunks of meat and steaming vegetables.

With Walter Sisulu in the prison yard on Robben Island in 1966.

The food was mouth-watering. The warders smiled as we refused to eat.

We then heard some strange news. The warders had gone on their own food boycott, refusing to eat in their cafeteria. They were not striking in support of us, but for better food and conditions for themselves. They felt that if we could protest in such a way, why couldn't they?

This was too much for the authorities. They gave the warders what they wanted, then they began discussions with the prisoners in the general section. The general prisoners declared victory and called off the strike. We stopped the next day. This was our first and most successful hunger-strike.

* * *

In the middle of the hunger-strike in July 1966, I had my second visit from Winnie. We had half an hour and much to talk about. We spoke about the education of the children, the health of my mother — which was not very good — and about our finances.

To get around talking about non-family matters, we used names whose meaning was clear to us. If, for example, I wanted to know about the ANC outside the country, I would ask, "How is the church?" Then I would ask about the priest and whether there were any new sermons. In this way, we managed to exchange a great deal of information.

As always, when the warder shouted, "Time up!" I thought only a few minutes had passed. I waited for Winnie to leave first so that she would not have to see me being led away. As she left, she whispered a goodbye, hiding her pain from the warders.

* * *

In the spring of 1966, the authorities began to change. They were no longer so cruel. A better understanding had developed between the prisoners and the warders.

But this came to a sudden end one morning in September. We were walking towards the shed for lunch, when a prisoner from the general section, who was wheeling a drum of food towards us, whispered, "Verwoerd is dead."

We were shocked — and so were the warders when they later heard the news. They took out their anger on us, and things were bad between us once again.

Twenty-four hours after the assassination of Verwoerd, a new warder by the name of van Rensburg was sent to the island. He was a big brute of a man who did not speak, but shouted. He had a reputation for being cruel to prisoners. His job was to make our lives as miserable as possible and he did this happily.

We soon gave him a nickname — we called him "Suitcase". Warders like to ask prisoners to carry their lunchboxes, which were called "suitcases". But we always refused to carry van Rensburg's suitcase — and that is how he got his new name.

Each day, over the next few months, Suitcase would charge one of us for something or another — mostly for no reason at all. Often, when our lunch arrived at the quarry and we would sit down to eat, Suitcase would decide to urinate near us as we ate.

One morning, Suitcase told us that the commanding officer, Major Kellerman, had given an order forbidding us to talk while we worked. We were not happy, because talking as we worked was one of our few pleasures.

A few hours later, during our lunch-break, Major Kellerman himself walked into the shed where we were eating. This was very unusual — we had never had such a high-ranking visitor in our lowly shed. He told us, in an embarrassed way, that his order had been a mistake and that we could carry on talking at the quarry, as long as we did so quietly.

We were pleased, but we knew that there was a reason for this change of heart. For the rest of the day we were not forced to work very hard. Even Suitcase was suddenly nice to us and said that he was going to withdraw all charges that he had made against us.

The following morning we were told by Suitcase that we would not be going to the quarry. Fifteen minutes later, Helen Suzman — all five feet, two inches of her — came through the door. She was with General Steyn, the Commissioner of Prisons.

Helen Suzman was one of the few Members of Parliament who cared about political prisoners. She had come to Robben Island to see for herself.

As she was introduced to each prisoner, she asked if he had any complaints. Each man replied in the same way, "I have many complaints, but our spokesman is Mr Mandela, at the end of the corridor."

Mrs Suzman was soon at my cell, introducing herself and shaking my hand firmly. We got down to business right away.

I told her about our need for better food, clothes and facilities for studying. I told her about the cruelty of the warders, especially Suitcase.

After inspecting our cells and chatting to the other prisoners, she left. We later heard that she had taken up our case in Parliament. Within a few weeks of her visit, Suitcase was transferred off the island.

* * *

The first years on the island were difficult times, both for those of us in prison and for the organisation outside. After Rivonia, all our underground structures were destroyed. Nearly all the senior leaders of the ANC were either in prison or in exile.

Oliver Tambo took charge of the organisation, leading it from outside the country.

The apartheid government had become more ruthless. It was supported by a growing and more brutal police force and army. Other countries, like the United States and Britain, did not really care about what was happening in South Africa.

But the winds of change were sweeping through the rest of Africa. In the late 1960s, liberation struggles were being fought in countries like Namibia, Mozambique and Zimbabwe. In 1967, the ANC formed an alliance with the Zimbabwean People's Army (ZAPU), under the leadership of Joshua Nkomo.

That year, a group of MK soldiers who had trained in Zambia and Tanzania crossed the Zambezi river into Rhodesia on their way back home. This first group of MK soldiers was known as the Luthuli Detachment. They were the spearhead of the armed struggle.

Justice Mpanza, one of the commanders of the Luthuli Detachment, was later imprisoned with us. He told us about the bravery of our soldiers. As a former commander-in-chief of MK, I felt very proud.

❆   ❆   ❆

In July 1967 we heard about the death of Chief Luthuli. He was hit by a train while walking near his home in Groutville. We grieved at the loss of our great leader, whose death left a big hole in the organisation.

But we were lucky to have a man like Oliver Tambo, who could step into the chief's shoes. Like Luthuli, he had a sharp mind yet was humble at the same time.

❆   ❆   ❆

In the spring of 1968 I was visited by my mother, whom I had not seen since the Rivonia Trial. She looked very old, and she had lost a lot of weight.

She had come all the way from the Transkei, together with my son, Makgatho, my daughter, Makaziwe, and my sister, Mabel. Because I had four visitors and they had come a long way, the authorities agreed to increase my visiting time from half an hour to 45 minutes.

I had not seen my son and daughter since before the trial, and they had grown up into adults without me. I looked at them with amazement and pride. Even though they had grown up, I'm afraid I still treated them like children. They might have changed, but I hadn't.

As always, the visit was over quickly. Usually I would spend hours thinking about a visit afterwards, treasuring every moment. But this time I could not stop worrying about my mother. I feared that I had seen her for the last time.

Several weeks later, after returning from the quarry, I was told to go and fetch a telegram from head office. It was from Makgatho, telling me that my mother had died from a heart attack. I immediately asked for permission to attend the funeral in the Transkei. This was refused.

It added to my grief that I was not able to bury my mother. It was my responsibility as her eldest child and only son.

* * *

In the early hours of the morning of 12 May 1969, the security police woke Winnie at our home in Orlando and detained her without charge under the Terrorism Act.

She was put into solitary confinement in Pretoria, where she was brutally questioned.

Six months later, Winnie and 22 others were charged under the Suppression of Communism Act for trying to rebuild the ANC.

Nothing hurt me more in prison than the thought that Winnie was in prison too. I often urged others not to worry about what they could not control. But now I was unable to take my own advice. I had many sleepless nights. What were they doing to my wife? Who was looking after my daughters? Who would pay the bills?

In October, 17 months after her arrest, the charges against her and the others were suddenly dropped, with no explanation. Within two weeks, she was banned again and placed under house arrest. She applied to visit me but was refused.

* * *

Not long after the death of my mother, I suffered another great loss. One cold morning in July 1969, I was called to the main office and given a telegram. It was from my younger son, Makgatho, and only one sentence long.

He informed me that his elder brother, my first and oldest son, Madiba Thembekile, whom we called Thembi, had been killed in a motor-car accident in the Transkei. Thembi was 25 years old and the father of two small children.

I do not have the words to express the sorrow and the loss I felt at that time. It left a hole in my heart that can never be filled.

I returned to my cell and lay on my bed. I do not know how long I stayed there. Some of the men looked in on me, but I could not talk.

Finally, Walter came to me and knelt beside my bed, and I handed him the telegram. He said nothing — he just held my hand. I do not know how long he remained with me. There is nothing one man can say to another at such a time.

Part Nine

Robben Island: Beginning to Hope

SLOWLY BUT SURELY, after many battles, conditions on the island began to improve.

By 1969, we had been given our own prison uniforms, instead of a different uniform each week. These uniforms actually fitted us and we were allowed to wash them ourselves.

Although African prisoners still did not get the same food as other prisoners, we were sometimes given bread in the mornings. But we were allowed to share our food anyway, so the differences did not really matter.

We were allowed to talk amongst ourselves at the quarry. If the commanding officer visited the quarry, the warders on duty would blow a whistle to warn us to pick up our tools.

* * *

Every Sunday morning, without fail, there was a prayer service which we had to attend.

During the first two years on the island, we were not allowed to leave our cells for the Sunday services. The minister would preach from the end of our corridor. But by our third year, services were held outside in the courtyard, which we preferred.

In those years, this was the only time that we were allowed to be in the courtyard, except for our half hour of exercise. Few of the men were religious, but no one minded the long sermons. We enjoyed being outside.

One of our first ministers was an Anglican priest by the name of Father Hughes. He was a Welshman who had served in the Second World War. He often gave bits of information and news in his sermons, which we greatly appreciated.

One Sunday, we were visited by a minister known as Brother September. One of our fellow prisoners volunteered to lead a prayer during the service. He asked us to close our eyes and pray. Everyone did so, including Brother September.

Eddie Daniels then tip-toed to the front, opened Brother September's briefcase, and pulled out the *Sunday Times*. It was the last time Brother September brought a newspaper with him to the island.

* * *

If Sunday was the highlight of the week, Christmas was the highlight of the year. It was the one day of the year when the authorities were kind to us.

We did not have to go to the quarry and we were allowed to buy some sweets. While we did not have a traditional Christmas meal, we were given an extra mug of coffee for supper.

We were allowed to organise a Christmas concert, hold competitions and put on a play.

The concert was our favourite event. It took place on Christmas morning in the courtyard. We would sing a mixture of African and English Christmas songs, and some protest songs as well. The warders did not seem to mind or know the difference; they enjoyed our singing as much as we did.

We also held a chess and draughts tournament, and played Scrabble and bridge. I took part in the draughts competition every year, and I sometimes won. The prize was usually a bar of chocolate.

* * *

Our lives suddenly changed for the worse in 1970. The island got a new commanding officer, Colonel Piet Badenhorst.

Badenhorst had a reputation as the cruellest officer in the whole prison service. His arrival meant one thing: the government felt that a stronger hand was needed on the island.

Our old warders were transferred off the island and replaced with Badenhorst's own men. They were younger and harder, and they made our lives a misery.

Within days of Badenhorst's arrival, our cells were raided and searched. Books and papers were confiscated, meals were cancelled without warning, and we were pushed and shoved on the way to the quarry.

Prisoners who asked to see their lawyers were given solitary confinement instead. Complaints were ignored. Visits were cancelled without any reason. The food got worse and our letters were cut up more than before.

Late one freezing-cold night in May, the warders came to our cells shouting, "Get up! Get up!" They ordered us to strip naked and line up against the wall of our cells. Then they searched our cells.

The warders were drunk, and they made fun of us as we stood there shivering. After an hour, Govan collapsed with chest pains. This scared the warders and they ordered us back to our cells.

We made a complaint about this incident, which was ignored. This was not the only time that something like this happened under Badenhorst's command.

* * *

We knew that we could not allow Badenhorst to get away with such behaviour. We smuggled messages to our people on the outside, asking for help to get rid of him. At the same time, we decided to meet with Badenhorst ourselves.

He agreed to meet us. At the meeting, we threatened him with work-stoppages, go-slows and hunger-strikes if he did not change his ways. He promised us nothing, but he said that he would think about what we had said.

Our messages to the outside world soon helped. Not long afterwards, three judges visited the island, together with the Commissioner of Prisons, General Steyn.

I told the judges about an assault by warders in the general section. Badenhorst wagged his finger in my face and said, "Be careful, Mandela. If you talk about things you haven't seen, you will get yourself into trouble. You know what I mean."

I ignored Badenhorst. "Gentlemen," I said to the judges, "you can see for yourselves the type of man we are dealing with as commanding officer. If he can threaten me here, in your presence, you can imagine what he does when you are not here."

I spent the rest of the meeting telling the judges about all our complaints. I have no idea what the judges said or did after the meeting. But Badenhorst treated us better after that.

Within three months of the judges' visit, we heard that Badenhorst was to be transferred off the island.

I met him for the last time a few days before he left. He told me that he would be leaving, and then he said, "I just want to wish you people good luck."

I was amazed. He had spoken the words like a human being. He showed a side of himself that we had never seen before.

I thought about this for a long time afterwards. Badenhorst was probably the worst commanding officer we had on the island. But that day in his office, he reminded me of a very important point: all men, even the most cold-blooded, have some decency, and if their hearts are touched, they can change.

* * *

One morning, we were told to get into the back of a truck instead of walking to the quarry. Fifteen minutes later, we saw the sea in front of us, shining in the morning light.

The senior officer explained that we had come to collect seaweed. This would be sent to Japan to be used as fertiliser.

After collecting the seaweed, we lined it up in rows on the beach. We loaded it into the back of a truck when it was dry.

The work did not seem too difficult on the first day, but in the coming weeks and months, we found it quite hard. We often cut our feet on the sharp rocks. Even so, we still preferred to work on the beach than at the quarry.

We enjoyed being out in nature, watching the gulls diving for fish in the sea and the seals playing in the waves. We laughed at the penguins, who strutted around like clumsy soldiers.

We ate well there. Each morning, we took a large drum of fresh water with us so that we could make a seafood stew with clams and mussels. We also caught crayfish and abalone which hid in the rocks.

Wilton Mkwayi was our chef who cooked the stew in the drum. When it was ready, the warders would join us and we would all sit down on the beach for a picnic lunch.

* * *

Robben Island became known as the "university". This was not only because of what we learned from books and our studies, but also because of what we learned from each other. We had our own "professors" who gave their own courses.

Walter, perhaps the greatest living historian of the ANC, gave a course on the history of the organisation. Kathy lectured on the history of the Indian struggle. Mac, who had studied in East Germany, gave a course on Marxism. I gave a course on political economy.

Walter's course was at the heart of all the learning. Many of the young ANC members who came to the island knew very little about the history of the organisation.

Before long, prisoners in the other sections asked to join our "university". We started a "correspondence course", with teachers and students smuggling lectures and questions back and forth to each other.

* * *

I was not only a part-time teacher — I was a part-time lawyer as well. I spent so many hours a week helping prisoners with their legal problems that I even thought about hanging a business name-plate outside my cell.

Many of the prisoners in the general section had been sentenced without having a lawyer to help them. They asked me to help them to make an appeal.

It was slow work. It was forbidden for prisoners to help other prisoners with legal problems, so consultations that should have lasted half an hour could take up to a year. Messages had to be smuggled between lawyer and client.

I enjoyed keeping my legal skills sharp and even won a few cases. These victories pleased me greatly.

I often did not meet the men I helped. When I did meet them, it came as a surprise. For example, a man who would be serving me pap for dinner would whisper a thank you for the work I had done for him.

* * *

Winnie continued to suffer at the hands of the police. In 1972, security police kicked down the door of our house in Orlando. They fired gunshots outside the house and threw bricks through the window.

Later, Winnie was charged for breaking her banning order. A friend had brought Zindzi and Zeni to visit her at the lawyer's office, where she was working. For this, she was sentenced to six months in Kroonstad Prison.

After Winnie was released, we worked out a plan for me to see Zindzi. She was 15 years old at the time. According to the rules, she could only visit me when she turned 16. The plan was for Winnie to change Zindzi's date of birth on her birth certificate. She did this easily enough, and Zindzi was given permission to visit me.

I had not seen Zindzi since she was three years old. I put on a fresh shirt that morning and took more trouble than usual with my appearance. I did not want to look like an old man for my youngest daughter.

When Zindzi arrived with her mother, I was delighted to see what a beautiful young woman she had become. Zindzi was shy at first, but I could see right away that she was a strong and fiery young woman, just like her mother had been.

I asked her questions about her life, her schooling and her friends. I told her of some of my early memories of her — like how I would sit her on my knee and play with her on Sunday mornings while her mother cooked the family lunch. Through the glass, I could see her fighting back the tears as I spoke.

*　*　*

For the whole time I was on the island, I never stopped thinking about trying to escape. Mac and Eddie were always thinking of ways to get out. Many of their plans were far too dangerous.

In 1974 Mac came up with a plan that we thought might work. He had recently visited a dentist in Cape Town, a kind-hearted man who had refused to treat him unless his leg-irons were removed.

Mac had noticed a window in the dentist's second-floor waiting room. From that window it was just a short drop to a small side-street. If we got to this street, he said, we could make a run for it.

Soon Mac, Wilton Mkwayi and myself had dentist appointments, and we were taken by boat to Cape Town. At the dentist, we demanded to have our leg-irons removed. The dentist agreed with us and the guards took them off.

Mac led us over to the window and pointed out the street that was to be our escape-route. But something about the street bothered him as he looked out. We were in the centre of Cape Town in the middle of the day, and yet the street was empty.

"It's a trap," Mac whispered. I, too, felt that something was not right.

Wilton said that we were talking nonsense. "Madiba, you're losing your nerve," he said. But I agreed with Mac, and the three of us ended up simply having our teeth examined. The dentist could not understand why I had come, because my teeth were fine.

* * *

We still celebrated birthdays, even though we could not buy presents or cakes. We would give an extra slice of bread or cup of coffee to the "birthday boy".

In 1975, when I turned 57, Walter and Kathy came to me with a plan that would make my sixtieth birthday more special. They suggested that I should write a book about my life. It could be published when I turned 60.

Walter said that my story would be an inspiration for young freedom fighters. It would remind the world of our struggle. I agreed to the idea immediately and I got started at once.

In the beginning, when I was still working at the quarry, I would rest after dinner until 10 p.m., and then write until breakfast.

It was exhausting to work at the quarry during the day, and to write for most of the night. After a while, I told the authorities that I was not feeling well and would not be going to the quarry. They did not seem to care. From then on, I was able to sleep for most of the day and write all night.

We started an assembly-line for the book. Each day, I passed on what I had written to Kathy and Walter. They read it and made comments. Then it was passed on to Laloo Chiba, who would spend the next night re-writing it in tiny short-hand. He managed to fit ten pages of my writing on to one small piece of paper.

Mac then hid Laloo's work inside the binding of the notebooks that he used for his studies. The plan was for Mac to smuggle out the book when he was released.

When I had finished, we divided my long, hand-written manuscript into three parts — two small and one large. We wrapped them in plastic before putting them in cocoa tins, which were then buried in the garden in the courtyard.

A few weeks later, just after our wake-up call, I heard the sound of picks and shovels. My heart sank as I realised that a work crew was digging in the area where the manuscript was buried. They were there to build a wall to separate us completely from the prisoners in the isolation section.

While washing, I told Walter and Kathy about the digging outside. When we went out into the courtyard for breakfast, the workers were ordered out of the area so that they could have no contact with us.

Walter, Kathy, Eddie and I walked over to the garden section and quickly managed to dig up the two small containers. There was not enough time to dig up the big one, but we felt sure that it would not be found because it was buried under a pipe. We gave the two small sections to Eddie, who was not going to the quarry that day, and asked him to destroy them as soon as possible.

When I returned from the quarry that afternoon, I was in for a big shock. The prisoners had dug a trench along the wall and had removed the pipe completely. They had surely found the manuscript.

Early the next morning, I was summoned to the office to see the commanding officer. He told me that they had found the manuscript. I tried to deny writing it, but it was of no use.

A short while later, Walter, Kathy and I were called to appear before the Deputy Commissioner of Prisons, General Rue. He told us that he was suspending our study privileges. We hoped that this would not last long. But as it turned out, we lost our study privileges for four years.

When Mac was released from prison, he smuggled out the tiny manuscript with him. After going into exile in London, he spent six months writing the manuscript out in full.

Many years later, once I was released from prison, I finished writing the book. And so it was published long after my sixtieth birthday. That birthday passed like any other.

* * *

In 1976, I was surprised with a visit from Jimmy Kruger, the Minister of Prisons at the time.

I had an idea why he was there. During this period, the government was doing its best to make its apartheid policy work.

I was not impressed with the man. He seemed to know nothing about the history of the ANC. But he was not there to learn about the ANC or to hear about our complaints.

He was there to make me an offer. If I recognised the Transkei — one of the homelands created by the apartheid government — and was willing to move there, I would be released from prison.

I listened to what he had to say, but I told him that I could never — and would never — support the homelands. I told him that I was from Johannesburg, and it was to Johannesburg that I would return.

He returned a month later with the same offer. Again, I gave him the same answer.

On 16 June 1976, 15 000 students gathered in Soweto to protest against being taught in Afrikaans.

* * *

16 June 1976 was a turning-point in the history of our struggle. News of what happened on that historic day reached us slowly on the island.

On that day, 15 000 students gathered in Soweto to protest against being taught in Afrikaans at school. Students did not want to learn in the language of their oppressors, and teachers did not want to teach in that language.

The police opened fire on the students without warning. Thirteen-year-old Hector Pieterson was the first to die. In the days and weeks that followed, hundreds of students were killed, both in Soweto and in other parts of the country where the protest had spread.

We learnt what had happened through whispered conversations. While we mourned the loss of so many young lives, we knew that the struggle had turned the corner. Thousands of young people were leaving South Africa to join MK.

By September, the isolation section of Robben Island was full of young men who had taken part in the uprising.

These young prisoners were different from anything we had seen before. They were angry and brave. They did not accept the rules of prison life, and the authorities did not know how to handle them.

It was clear that these young lions thought that we older prisoners were soft. After so many years of being called radical revolutionaries, it was not a nice feeling for us to be seen in such a way.

* * *

I was walking with the commanding officer one day, when we saw a young prisoner being interviewed by a prison official.

The young man, who was no more than 18, was wearing his prison cap in the presence of senior officers. This was against prison rules. He did not stand up when the commanding officer entered, which was also against the rules.

When the major asked him to remove his cap, the young man looked at the major and said, "What for?" I could hardly believe what I had just heard.

When the major told him it was against regulations, the man said, "Why do you have this regulation? What is the purpose of it?"

This was too much for the major. He turned around and marched out of the room, saying, "Mandela, you talk to him." But I chose not to interfere and simply bowed my head at the prisoner to let him know that I was on his side.

* * *

The authorities paid less attention to us because they had their hands full with the young lions.

We were in the second year of a go-slow strike on the quarry and were demanding an end to all manual labour.

We felt that we should be allowed to do something more useful with our days, like studying or learning a trade.

The authorities announced an end to manual labour in 1977. This was a victory for us. I could now spend my days reading, writing letters, talking to my comrades and doing some legal work.

I also had time to do what I loved — gardening and playing tennis.

For years the prison authorities would not allow me to have my own garden. But they finally gave in, and I made a small garden against the far wall in the courtyard.

I started by growing tomatoes, chillies and onions. These were strong plants that could easily grow in the rocky and dry soil. In the beginning the harvests were poor, but they soon improved and I was growing big tomatoes and onions.

I soon began to order books on gardening and studied different ways of growing vegetables. I learnt by trial and error.

A garden is one of the few things in prison that one can control. To plant a seed, watch it grow, to tend it and then harvest it gave me a feeling of simple happiness. Being in charge of a small piece of earth was like having a small taste of freedom.

I saw my garden as a symbol of my life. Like a gardener, a leader must take responsibility for what he grows — he plants the seeds and watches them grow and then harvests the results.

※　※　※

Right from the start, I had told the International Red Cross and other visitors that we needed time and facilities for proper exercise. But it was only in the mid 1970s that we got equipment for volleyball and table tennis.

One of the warders had the idea of making the courtyard into a tennis court. Prisoners from the general section painted the cement floor green, drew white lines and put up a net. We soon had Wimbledon in our front yard!

I was one of the first in our section to play tennis regularly. I had a strong forehand but a weak backhand. I liked to play from the back of the court, rushing to the front only when I could be sure of hitting a winner.

* * *

In August, two months after the Soweto uprising, Winnie was detained once again. As a member of the Black Parents' Association in Soweto, she had tried to help the students in their struggle. She was held for five months in the Fort in Johannesburg, without being charged. When she was released, she was still not left alone.

On 16 May 1977, police cars and a truck pulled up outside the house in Orlando West and began loading furniture and clothing into the back of the truck. This time she was not being arrested or detained — she was being banished to the small township in Brandfort in the Free State, 250 miles south-east of Johannesburg.

Winnie and Zindzi were dumped in front of a three-roomed shack in Brandfort's African township. It was a bleak and poor place. They knew nobody there, and could not even speak Sotho, the language of the local people.

Life was hard for my wife and daughter at house number 802, Brandfort. They had no heat, no toilet, and no running water. And the police still did not leave them alone. They watched them all the time and would burst into the house without knocking.

But Winnie is not the sort of person who gives up. Before long, she had the people behind her. She organised food for the people in the township from Operation Hunger, started a crèche for the children, and raised money for a clinic.

* * *

In 1978, Zeni, my second-youngest daughter, and my first child with Winnie, married Prince Thumbumuzi, a son of King Sobhuza of Swaziland.

They came to visit me that winter, bringing with them their new baby daughter.

Zeni was now given diplomatic privileges because she was a member of the Swazi royal family. This meant that she could visit me whenever she wanted, and we could meet in the consulting room face to face, without the usual thick walls and glass that normally separated a prisoner from his visitors.

I waited for them nervously. When they came into the room, it was a wonderful moment for me.

I stood up, and when Zeni saw me, she ran over to hug me. I had not held my daughter since she was about her own daughter's age.

I then hugged my new son, and he handed me my tiny granddaughter. I took her and held her close to me for the rest of the visit. To hold a baby, so soft in my rough hands — hands that for too long had held only picks and shovels — was such a great joy. I don't think a man was ever happier to hold a baby than I was that day.

It was my duty — as the grandfather — to give the child a name. I chose the name Zaziwe — which means "hope". The name had a special meaning for me. During all my years in prison, I had never lost hope — and now I never would. I believed deeply that this child would be part of a new generation of South Africans, for whom apartheid would be a distant memory. That was my dream.

* * *

Winnie sent me a photograph album when the authorities allowed us to keep photographs of our families in the early 1970s.

When I received a photograph of Winnie, the children or the grandchildren, I would carefully paste them into the album. I treasured this album — it was the one way I could see those I loved whenever I wanted.

In the early days, the warders would often come into my cell and confiscate pictures of Winnie. They did this even though I was allowed to keep the photographs. When they stopped doing this, I built up a thick album with pictures of my whole family.

Other prisoners often asked me to lend them my album. Some of these prisoners — mostly from F and G sections — never got visits or even letters. The album was a window to the outside world for these men.

Sometimes, men would ask me for a single photograph, rather than the whole album. I remember the time when a young fellow, who was bringing us food, took me aside and said, "Madiba, I would like a photograph."

I told him that I would let him have one. "When?" he asked, rather impatiently. I told him that I would try to send it that weekend.

He seemed happy with this, and began to walk away. But suddenly he turned around and said, "Look, don't send me a photograph of the old lady. Send me one of the young girls, Zindzi or Zeni — remember, not the old lady!"

※　※　※

The authorities started their own radio station in 1978, 15 years after we began demanding the right to receive news. Every day, a summary of the day's news was read over the prison intercom.

We only heard the news that the government wanted us to hear. But for us, some news was better than no news at all. We became good at reading between the lines and guessing what news was being left out.

That year, we heard on the intercom that John Vorster had resigned, and that P W Botha was the country's new Prime Minister. We did not know much about Botha, except that he had been the Minister of Defence for a long time. He was known as a hard man.

Even before the prison radio we had heard about some very important events, like the victories of the liberation struggles in Mozambique and Angola in 1975. The tide was turning our way.

* * *

In 1980, we were given permission to buy newspapers. But as always, there was a catch.

Only A-group prisoners were allowed newspapers — and they were not allowed to share them with the other prisoners. And when the newspapers came to us, they were full of holes, having first gone to the prison censors.

One story I was not able to read was the one published in the Johannesburg *Sunday Post* in 1980. The headline read: "Free Mandela!"

The idea for a campaign to free me and all the other political prisoners had come from Oliver Tambo and the ANC.

The newspaper could not print any of the words I had written or spoken. Nor could it publish any pictures of me. But the campaign caught the imagination of the people — both at home and abroad.

But it was not only the campaign that gave us fresh hope. The ANC was getting stronger and more popular every day.

In June, MK soldiers set off a huge explosion at the Sasolburg oil refinery. Attacks followed at police and power stations around the country, and at Voortrekkerhoogte, a big military base outside Pretoria.

* * *

One day, in March 1982, I was visited in my cell by the commanding officer and a number of other officials. This was very unusual. The commanding officer did not often visit prisoners in their cells.

"Mandela," he said, "I want you to pack your things." When I asked him why, he said that they were transferring me. He could not tell me where, except to say that he had orders from Pretoria.

He then went to the cells of Walter, Raymond Mhlaba and Andrew Mlangeni and told them the same thing.

We were given large cardboard boxes to pack our things in. I had been on the island for more than 18 years, but it took me less than half an hour to pack.

We were not given a chance to say goodbye to our comrades and friends. Within minutes, we were on a ferry to Cape Town.

There we were put into a truck without windows, and the four of us stood in the dark for the journey of over an hour.

Finally, the truck stopped and the back doors swung open. I asked a guard where we were.

"Pollsmoor Prison," he said.

Part Ten

Talking with the Enemy

POLLSMOOR PRISON lies on the edge of a wealthy white suburb called Tokai, a few miles south east of Cape Town. It is surrounded by beautiful mountains and vineyards. But all this beauty meant little to those of us behind the high concrete walls.

Pollsmoor had two faces. It had modern buildings where the prison officials lived, and dirty, old buildings where the prisoners were kept.

The four of us were kept separately from the other prisoners, and we were treated differently. We were given the whole of the third floor of the prison block to ourselves. It was large and clean, with a separate toilet and showers. We were given proper beds with sheets and towels. This was a great luxury for men who had spent the last 18 years sleeping on mats on the floor.

We were soon joined by Ahmed Kathrada, and later by a young lawyer and ANC member, Patrick Maqubela. Our quarters led out to an L-shaped veranda. We were allowed out on to the veranda all day, except between twelve and two, when the warders had their lunch.

The food was also much better. After years of eating pap three times a day, the meat and vegetables that we got at Pollsmoor were a treat. Compared to Robben Island, Pollsmoor was like a five-star hotel!

* * *

Soon after arriving at Pollsmoor, I asked for permission to

start a garden on the roof of the building. I requested — and received — sixteen 44-gallon drums. These were cut in half to make 32 giant flowerpots.

Each morning, I put on a straw hat and gloves, and worked in the garden for two hours. My garden soon looked like a small farm. Every Sunday I gave fresh vegetables to the prison kitchen, so that they could cook a special meal for the general prisoners. I also gave vegetables to the warders, who brought big bags to take away the fresh produce.

* * *

It was much easier for Winnie to visit me at Pollsmoor, and she came soon after I got there. The visitors' room was bigger and more modern than the one at Robben Island. It had a big window and a proper microphone.

A warder, Warrant Officer James Gregory, watched over my visits. He was a decent man and treated Winnie with respect. Instead of saying, "Time up," he would say, "Mrs Mandela, you have five more minutes."

The launch of the United Democratic Front in Cape Town in October 1983.

In May 1984, Winnie and Zeni came to visit me. But this time, instead of taking me to the usual visiting area, Warrant Officer Gregory took me to a separate room which had a small table and no dividers. He told me that the authorities had changed the rules. I would now be allowed "contact visits".

A few minutes later, Winnie came through the door. Suddenly she was in my arms. It was a moment I had dreamt about a thousand times. I held her close to me for what seemed like a life-time. We were still and silent, except for the sound of our heartbeats. It had been 21 years since I had even touched my wife's hand.

*   *   *

The struggle reached new heights in the early 1980s. In 1981, the South African Defence Force raided ANC offices in Maputo and killed 13 of our people. The same month, they attacked Maseru, killing 42 people, including women and children.

MK hit back, setting off bombs at the Koeberg nuclear power plant and many other military and apartheid targets around the country.

In 1983, the United Democratic Front was formed. The UDF was made up of over 600 anti-apartheid organisations. It was created to fight the government's plan to create a new tricameral parliament.

This plan was to give coloured and Indian people seats in their own separate parliaments. This would bring them into the government, and divide them from Africans. It was also a way of fooling the outside world into thinking that the government was moving away from apartheid.

The UDF had strong links with the ANC, which at this time was growing more popular by the day. The struggle against apartheid was being joined by countries all over the world which were now refusing to do business with South

Africa. The apartheid government was under more pressure than ever before.

✻   ✻   ✻

On 31 January 1985, P W Botha stood up in parliament and made an offer to me, and to all other political prisoners. He would free us if we "unconditionally rejected violence as a political instrument". He then went on to say, "It is therefore not the government that stands in the way of Mr Mandela's freedom. It is he himself."

This offer of freedom — with conditions — was not the first. This was the sixth time I had got such an offer in the past ten years.

Once again, I could not agree to be released with conditions. On Sunday, 10 February 1985, my daughter Zindzi read my reply to P W Botha at a UDF rally at Orlando Stadium in Soweto.

I believed that Botha had made the offer to try to divide me from my comrades in the ANC. So I began by saying that I would be a loyal member of the ANC until the day I died. I said that Botha should show that he was different from the leaders who came before him by bringing an end to apartheid. I ended by saying:

> What freedom am I being offered while the organisation of the people remains banned? What freedom am I being offered when I may be arrested on a pass offence? What freedom am I being offered to live my life as a family man with my dear wife who remains in banishment in Brandfort? What freedom am I being offered when I must ask for permission to live in an urban area? ... What freedom am I being offered when my very South African citizenship is not respected?

118

Only free men can negotiate. Prisoners cannot enter into contracts ... I cannot and will not give any undertaking at a time when I and you, the people, are not free. Your freedom and mine cannot be separated.

* * *

In 1985 I found myself in Volks Hospital in Cape Town. My prostate gland was enlarged and I needed an operation.

I was visited by Winnie before the operation. My next visitor was more of a surprise. It was none other than Kobie Coetsee, the Minister of Justice.

He behaved as if he was visiting an old friend — and I acted as if this was the most normal thing in the world. But I was amazed. I realised what Coetsee's visit meant: the government was slowly beginning to understand that it had to talk to the ANC.

Brigadier Munro, the commanding officer of Pollsmoor, came to fetch me from the hospital several days later. I was suspicious — commanding officers do not often fetch prisoners from hospital.

On the way back, Brigadier Munro said, "Mandela, we are not taking you back to your friends now. From now on, you are going to be alone."

When I asked why, he said he did not know — he had been given instructions from headquarters in Pretoria.

Back at Pollsmoor, I was given a new cell on the ground floor. It had three rooms and a separate toilet. For a prisoner, this was like living in a palace. There was only one problem — it was damp and there was little natural light.

I was not happy to be separated from my comrades and I missed my garden and the sunny veranda on the third floor. But over the next few days and weeks, I realised that being alone was not such a bad thing. In fact, it was an opportunity for me to do something I had been thinking about doing for a long time — beginning discussions with the government.

I now realised that if the government and the ANC did not talk soon, the country would sink into a long and bitter war. Thousands, if not millions, of lives would be lost. The time had come to talk.

I decided to tell no one what I was about to do. Not my comrades upstairs, nor those in Lusaka. There are times when a leader must move ahead of the flock, go off in a new direction, feeling sure that he is leading his people down the right road.

※ ※ ※

Within a few weeks of my move, I wrote to Kobie Coetsee to suggest that we begin talking. I received no reply. I wrote once more, and again I heard nothing.

In May 1986, I was visited by the Eminent Persons Group. This group, led by General Obasanjo of Nigeria, was sent by the British Commonwealth on a fact-finding mission to South Africa. After they saw me, the group was to meet with the cabinet. I saw this as another opportunity to send a signal to the government that the time had come to begin discussions.

Brigadier Munro came to see me a few days before I met the Eminent Persons Group. He brought a tailor with him, saying that he wanted me to be dressed properly for the meeting. The very next day, I had a pinstriped suit that fitted me like a glove. I was also given a shirt, tie, shoes, socks and underwear.

When the commander saw me in my new outfit, he smiled and said, "Mandela, you look like a Prime Minister, not a prisoner."

※ ※ ※

Kobie Coetsee and General Willemse, the Commissioner of Prisons, arrived with the Eminent Persons Group, but left soon after the meeting started. I invited them to stay, saying I had nothing to hide. They left anyway, but before they did, I told them that it was time the ANC and the government sat down and talked.

The group wanted to know about my views on violence and how I saw a future South Africa. I told them that I still supported the Freedom Charter, which committed the ANC to democracy and human rights. I told them that violence was not the answer to the country's problems. I said that the ANC might agree to suspend the armed struggle if the government pulled its troops out of the townships.

The group said that they would visit me again. I was hopeful that its work would lead to talks between the government and the ANC.

But it was not to be. The day before I was to meet the Eminent Persons Group again, the South African Defence Force attacked ANC bases in Botswana, Zambia and Zimbabwe. The group felt that they were unable to continue with their work, and they left South Africa immediately.

Once again, my efforts to get discussions going had failed.

* * *

On 12 June 1986, the government declared a State of Emergency. This was their way of dealing with the anger of the people, which had now reached boiling point.

Still, I did not give up hope of getting discussions going. I wrote to General Willemse and asked him to come and see me. I was told a few days later that he would be in Cape Town and would meet with me that weekend.

We did not meet in the visiting area, but instead I was taken to his house at Pollsmoor. We got down to business right away.

I told him that I wanted to meet the Minister of Justice, so that I could try again to get talks going between the government and the ANC.

The general thought for a second, and said, "It just so happens that the Minister of Justice is in Cape Town. Perhaps you can see him."

The general picked up the phone and phoned Coetsee, whose answer was short and sweet. "Bring him round," he said.

Minutes later, I was in the general's car, driving to the minister's house in Cape Town. I was still dressed in my prison clothes.

The minister greeted me warmly. We spoke for three hours, sitting in comfortable chairs in his lounge. He asked me many questions — for example, under what circumstances would the ANC give up the armed struggle? How would minorities be protected in a new South Africa?

Towards the end of the meeting, he asked me what the next step was. I told him I wanted to meet the State President, and the Minister of Foreign Affairs, Pik Botha.

Coetsee made notes and said that he would pass on my request. We then shook hands, and I was driven back to my cell at Pollsmoor Prison.

I felt very hopeful. But once again, nothing happened. Weeks, and then months, passed, and I heard nothing from Coetsee. I decided to write him another letter.

❆　❆　❆

Although I did not get a reply from Kobie Coetsee, there were other signs that the government was preparing me for a new role.

On the day before Christmas, Lieutenant Colonel Gawie Marx, the deputy commander of Pollsmoor, came into my cell after breakfast and said, "Mandela, would you like to see the city?"

I wasn't sure what he had in mind, but thought that there was no harm in saying yes. We walked through the 15 metal doors between my cell and the entrance to the prison, and got into his car.

We drove to Cape Town on the road that runs along the coast. In the city, we drove around, and it was an incredible feeling to watch ordinary people doing ordinary things in the world: old men sitting in the sun, women doing their shopping, people walking their dogs. It is these ordinary things that one misses in prison. I felt like a tourist in a strange land.

The colonel took me out a few more times during the next few months. We not only drove through the city, but we also went to beaches and the lovely cool mountains around Cape Town.

Later, I was taken out by younger warders, who took me quite far out. We walked on beaches and drank tea at cafes. I often wondered if people recognised me, but no one ever did. The last picture of me had been taken in 1964.

* * *

I began talking again to Kobie Coetsee again in 1987. We met several times at his house. Later that year, the government made its first real proposal.

Coetsee said that the government wanted to appoint a committee of senior officials to have private discussions with me. He himself would head the committee, and it would include General Willemse, the Commissioner of Prisons, Fanie van der Merwe, Director General of the prisons department, and Dr Niel Barnard, who was head of the National Intelligence Service.

After thinking about the proposal, I accepted. But I decided that I had to do three things first: I needed to talk to my comrades on the third floor, write to Oliver Tambo in Lusaka, and send a letter to P W Botha.

I decided that I would not tell my comrades about the committee. Instead, I would simply ask how they felt about beginning talks with the government.

I was only allowed to meet my comrades one by one. Walter was not against the idea, but he did say that he

123

would have preferred it if the government had started talks instead of me. I replied that if he was not against negotiations, what did it matter who started the talking? Walter could see that my mind was made up, and he said that he would not stop me. He only hoped that I knew what I was doing.

Raymond Mhlaba was more encouraging. "Madiba, what have you been waiting for?" he said. "We should have started this years ago." Andrew Mlangeni gave me a similar answer.

But Kathy was completely against the idea. He felt that if we were the ones who pushed for talks, it would seem as if we were giving in. But he said that he would not stand in my way, even though he believed I was going down the wrong path.

* * *

Not long after this, I received a note from Oliver Tambo, which was smuggled to me by one of my lawyers.

The note was short and to the point. He said that he knew that I had been separated from my colleagues and had been alone for some time. What was I discussing with the government? I could tell that he thought I was making a mistake.

I replied that I was doing one thing and one thing alone: I was trying to set up a meeting between the National Executive of the ANC and the South African government. I said the time had come for talks. I would not let the organisation down.

I knew that Oliver would understand as soon as he read the letter that I was writing to P W Botha.

* * *

The first meeting between myself and the senior government officials took place in May 1988, at an officers' club in the grounds of Pollsmoor Prison.

The first meeting was stiff, but we talked more freely in later meetings. I met them almost every week for a few months. After that we met only when we needed to.

In the beginning, I spent a lot of time explaining the history of the ANC. I explained why the ANC's views on certain issues were different from the government's views. Then we spoke about what worried the government: the armed struggle, the ANC's alliance with the Communist Party, majority rule and what would happen to minorities, and the fear that an ANC government would take over — or nationalise — some industries when we came to power.

We spent a number of months talking about the armed struggle. They said the ANC had to give up the armed struggle before the government would agree to negotiations — and before I could meet P W Botha. I said that the state was responsible for violence. If the state used peaceful means, the ANC would use peaceful means. "It is up to you, not us, to renounce violence," I said.

* * *

I had been suffering from a bad cough for a while, which would not go away. I had complained about the dampness of my cell, but nothing had been done about it.

One day, during a meeting with my lawyer I suddenly felt ill and vomited. A few days later, after being examined by a physician, I was told to get dressed. They told me I was being taken to a hospital in Cape Town.

I was examined there by a doctor who told me that I had water on the lung. He decided to operate immediately.

I woke up from the operation to find the doctor standing next to me. He told me that I had tuberculosis. It was still in the early stages, so there was no damage to the lung. The doctor said that I would be better within two months, with proper treatment. He agreed that it was probably the damp cell that had caused the illness.

* * *

I spent the next six weeks being treated at Tygerberg Hospital. Then I was moved to the Constantiaberge Clinic near Pollsmoor Prison. I was the first black patient ever to be admitted there.

At Constantiaberge I again began to meet Kobie Coetsee and the secret committee. Coetsee told me that he wanted to put me in a place that would be half-way between prison and freedom. He did not explain what he had in mind, but I knew that it was a step in the right direction.

* * *

On the evening of 9 December 1988, Major Marais came into the room and told me to prepare to leave. He did not say where I would be going.

We left in a rush, and made our way to the Paarl Valley, in the heart of the Cape wine-growing country. After an hour, we got to the entrance of the place that was to be my new home: Victor Verster Prison.

We drove down a winding dirt road inside the prison gates until we came to a cottage. It was set behind a concrete wall and shaded by tall fir trees.

Inside, I found a large lounge next to a large kitchen, with an even larger bedroom at the back. There was not much furniture, but it was comfortable.

The next morning, I discovered a swimming pool in the back yard, and two smaller bedrooms. I walked outside and admired the trees that shaded the house and kept it cool. The only thing that spoilt the picture was the razor wire on top of the walls, and guards at the entrance to the house. But it was still a lovely place: a half-way house between prison and freedom.

* * *

I was given my own cook, Warrant Officer Swart. He was a tall, quiet Afrikaner, who had once been a warder on Robben Island. He was a decent fellow and he became like a brother to me.

He arrived at seven in the morning and left at four, and would make breakfast, lunch and supper. He was a wonderful cook and when I had visitors, he would cook delicious meals. When I was later allowed visits from comrades in the ANC and the UDF, I often teased them that they only came for the food.

*　*　*

The meetings with the committee carried on, but we kept coming back to the same things that stopped us from moving forward: the armed struggle, the Communist Party and majority rule. I continued to ask for a face-to-face meeting with P W Botha.

At this time, the authorities allowed me some contact with my comrades at Pollsmoor and Robben Island, as well as with the ANC in Lusaka. This was important. I did not want to go too far ahead of my comrades and find that I was alone.

In March 1989, I sent the letter to P W Botha. In the letter, I proposed a two-stage plan: that we first begin with talks about getting the conditions right for negotiations, and that we then move on to the real negotiations.

I told him that I hoped that he would agree without delay.

*　*　*

But there was a delay. In January, P W Botha suffered a stroke. The following month, he resigned as head of the National Party, but stayed on as President.

Political violence at home and international pressure continued to increase. Political detainees all over the country held hunger-strikes. This forced the government to release over 900 of them.

In 1989, the Congress of South African Trade Unions (COSATU) and the UDF formed an alliance. They started a defiance campaign to challenge apartheid.

That July, for my seventy-first birthday, I was visited at the cottage at Victor Verster by my whole family. It was the first time I had ever had my wife and children all in one place, and it was a grand and happy occasion. The only pain I felt was knowing that I had missed out on this pleasure for so many years.

* * *

On 4 July, I was visited by General Willemse who told me that I would be taken to see President Botha the next day.

Once again, I was visited by a tailor, and by that afternoon, I had a new suit, tie and shoes.

At half-past five the next morning, Major Marais, the commanding officer of Victor Verster, came to fetch me. He looked at me, and then shook his head from side to side.

"No, Mandela, your tie," he said. I had realised when I was getting dressed that morning that I had forgotten how to put on a tie. But I did my best, and hoped that no one would notice. I was wrong. Major Marais stood behind me, undid my knot, and tied a double Windsor knot. He stood back and nodded his head. "Much better," he said.

We drove to General Willemse's house at Pollsmoor Prison, where we had breakfast. After that we went on to the President's office at Tuynhuys, which we entered through an underground garage.

Outside PW's office, we were met by Kobie Coetsee, Dr Niel Barnard and several prison officials.

While we were waiting, Dr Barnard saw that my shoelaces were not properly tied. He bent down to tie them for me. I realised that they were all very nervous. P W Botha did not have the nickname "die Groot Krokodil" ("the Big Crocodile") for nothing!

The door opened and I expected the worst. But to my surprise, he greeted me warmly. He was very polite and friendly.

After posing for a photograph of the two of us shaking hands, we sat down at a long table, together with Willemse, Coetsee and Barnard. We did not speak about the important things. We spoke instead about South African history and culture.

We spoke about the Afrikaner Rebellion of 1914, which I compared to the struggle against apartheid. There were many similarities between the two struggles, I said. But the others around the table did not agree.

The meeting lasted less than half an hour. At the end, I asked Mr Botha to release all political prisoners, including myself, without conditions. Mr Botha said that he could not do that. That was the only uncomfortable moment in the meeting.

When the meeting ended, Mr Botha stood up, shook my hand, and told me what a pleasure it had been. I thanked him, and left the way I had come.

*   *   *

P W Botha resigned as State President in August 1989, a little more than a month after our meeting. The following day, F W de Klerk was sworn in as acting State President. He said that his government wanted peace, and that he would talk with any group that wanted peace too. I immediately wrote to him to ask for a meeting.

*   *   *

On 10 October 1989, President de Klerk announced that Walter Sisulu and my other comrades from the Rivonia trial were to be released. That morning, I was visited by Walter, Kathy, Ray and Andrew, and I was able to say goodbye.

Five days later, they were released from Johannesburg Prison. I knew that I would not be far behind.

In early December, I was told that I would be meeting de Klerk later in the month. I wrote a letter to him, similar to the one I had written to P W Botha. I told him that his words and actions had given millions of people hope that a new South Africa was about to be born.

I said that I supported the Harare Declaration drawn up by the ANC. This document said that talks could only begin after the government had released all political prisoners, lifted the bans on all organisations and people, ended the State of Emergency, and removed all the troops from the townships.

꙰ ꙰ ꙰

On the morning of 13 December, I was again taken to Tuynhuys. I met de Klerk in the same room where I had had tea with P W Botha.

The first thing I noticed about de Klerk was that he listened to what I had to say. He was different from other National Party leaders. The others only heard what they wanted to hear when they spoke to black leaders.

I told him that I was against the Nationalist Party's new policy of "group rights". I said that it was simply a way of bringing apartheid back in through the back door.

I then spoke about my release. I said that the government must unban the ANC, or I would be working for an illegal organisation when I was freed. "Then," I said, "you must simply re-arrest me after I walk through those gates."

De Klerk said he would think about what I had said, but he could make no promises. But I left the meeting with new hope, believing that de Klerk was different from other National Party leaders. I wrote to the ANC in Lusaka and told my people that I believed de Klerk was a man we could do business with.

* * *

On 2 February 1990, F W de Klerk stood before Parliament to make the opening speech. And in that speech, he did what no other South African president had ever done: he broke down the building blocks of apartheid and laid the foundations for a democratic South Africa.

He lifted the bans on the ANC, the PAC, the South African Communist Party, and 31 other illegal organisations. Political prisoners were to be freed, the death penalty was suspended, and parts of the State of Emergency were lifted. "The time for negotiation has arrived," he said.

Our world had changed overnight. After 40 years of being a banned organisation, the ANC was now a legal organisation. For the first time in almost 30 years, my picture and my words could now appear in South African newspapers and on television.

But it was not all good news. The ANC was not happy that Mr de Klerk had not lifted the State of Emergency completely. Nor had he ordered all the troops out of the townships.

* * *

A week after Mr de Klerk's speech in Parliament, I was told that I would be going to Tuynhuys again. I arrived at six o'clock in the evening and met a smiling Mr de Klerk. He told me that he was going to release me from prison the following day.

This came as a surprise. Although I was expecting to be released, I did not think it would happen so soon.

I wanted to leave prison as soon as I could, but I knew that it would not be wise. I thanked Mr de Klerk, and asked if I could be freed a week later, so that my family and organisation could be prepared for my release.

Mr de Klerk could not believe my response. He carried on telling me about the plan for my release, as if he had not heard me. He said that the government would fly me to Johannesburg and release me there.

Before he could carry on, I stopped him again. I told him that I wanted to walk out of the gates of Victor Verster. I wanted to be able to thank those who had looked after me there, and I wanted to greet the people of Cape Town. Though I was from Johannesburg, Cape Town had been my home for nearly 30 years.

I would make my way back to Johannesburg when I chose to, and not when the government wanted me to. "Once I am free," I said, "I will look after myself."

Mr de Klerk was not happy. He excused himself to consult with his colleagues. He came back and said that the plan could not be changed. I stood my ground, and again he excused himself. Neither of us at the time thought it strange that the jailer wanted to release a prisoner from jail, but the prisoner was asking not to be released.

He came back with a compromise. They had to release me the next day because the government had already told the press. But I would be allowed to leave from Victor Verster. I agreed.

Mr de Klerk poured some whisky for us to drink in celebration. I raised the glass in a toast, but only pretended to drink. Such spirits are too strong for me.

I did not get back to my cottage until shortly before midnight. I immediately sent word to my comrades in Cape Town to tell them that I was going to be released the next day.

I sent a message to Winnie and telephoned Walter in Johannesburg. Then members of the National Reception Committee arrived to help me to write the speech I would give the next day. They left in the early hours of the morning. Although I was excited, I had no trouble falling asleep.

Part Eleven

Freedom

I WOKE UP AT FOUR-THIRTY on 11 February, after just a few hours' sleep. I did a little bit of exercise, washed and ate my breakfast. I behaved as if it was just another day in prison.

I tried not to think too much about the day ahead. Instead, I thought about all the many things I had to do before my release.

Members of the ANC and the UDF visited me again. We had a lot to talk about. We needed to decide where I would make my first speech and where I would sleep that night.

In the end, we decided that I would first speak to the people of Cape Town at the Grand Parade in the city centre. From there I would go to the home of Archbishop Desmond Tutu in Bishopscourt, where I would spend my first night of freedom.

※　※　※

The time for my release was set for three o'clock in the afternoon. But Winnie and Walter did not arrive from Johannesburg until after two o'clock.

Shortly before four o'clock, we left the cottage in a small motorcade. Our car stopped a few hundred metres inside the prison gates, and Winnie and I got out. We made our way slowly towards the huge crowd who were waiting outside.

As I walked out of the prison gates, I raised my right fist, and there was a big roar from the crowd. I had not been able to do that for 27 years, and I felt a rush of strength and joy.

I felt that my life was starting over again at the age of 71. My 10 000 days of imprisonment were over at last.

* * *

Getting to the Grand Parade in Cape Town was a lot harder than we thought. As we got closer, we could see an enormous crowd. The crowd surrounded the car, and banged on the windows, the boot and the bonnet. Inside, it sounded like a big hailstorm.

Then people jumped on the car and started to shake it. I began to worry and feared that the crowd might kill us with their love. We stayed inside the car for more than an hour, imprisoned by our own supporters.

Finally, the marshals cleared a path for us, and our driver drove off in a panic. I asked him where he was going — he said he did not know.

After a long drive around Cape Town, we made our way back to the Grand Parade. It was almost dusk when I was led up to the top floor of the City Hall. I walked out on the balcony and saw a great sea of people before me.

I raised my fist to the crowd and they responded with an enormous cheer. *"Amandla!"* I shouted, and they answered with a huge *"Ngawethu!"*

When the crowd settled down, I took out my speech and slowly began to read:

> Friends, comrades and fellow South Africans. I greet you all in the name of peace, democracy and freedom for all! I stand here before you not as a prophet but as a humble servant of you, the people. Your tireless and heroic sacrifices have made it possible for me to be here today. I therefore place the remaining years of my life in your hands.

I thanked all the people from all over the world for

campaigning for my release. I saluted Oliver Tambo and the ANC, and the many organisations in the country who had fought against apartheid.

I spoke of my family's pain and suffering, which I said had been far greater than my own.

I explained my negotiations with the government. I said that I believed it was possible to have peace and justice in the country. But I told the people that the struggle was not yet over. We should walk the last mile together, I said.

* * *

Thousands of people lined the streets to greet me as we drove to Archbishop Desmond Tutu's house.

I hugged the Archbishop warmly. He had inspired the whole nation with his words and courage, and he had given people hope during the darkest times.

Members of my family and friends were waiting at the house to greet us. Soon after I arrived, I was told there was a phone call for me from Sweden. I knew immediately who it was. To hear Oliver's voice after all those years gave me great joy.

Oliver was recovering from a stroke that he had suffered in August 1989. We agreed to meet as soon as possible.

* * *

Winnie and I had hoped to spend a few relaxing days in Cape Town before travelling to Johannesburg. But we were told that the people in Johannesburg were becoming restless and that I should go there at once.

We flew to Johannesburg that evening, but I could not go home to Orlando West. I wanted to spend my second night of freedom under my own roof, but we were told that thousands of people had surrounded our house. It would not be safe. Instead, Winnie and I stayed at the home of an ANC supporter in Johannesburg.

The following day, we flew in a helicopter to the First National Bank stadium in Soweto.

The stadium was overflowing with people: 120 000 had squeezed into every inch of space. I told the people how happy I was to be back among them:

> Today, my return to Soweto fills my heart with joy. At the same time, I also return with a deep sense of sadness. Sadness to learn that you are still suffering under an inhuman system. The housing shortage, the schools crisis, unemployment and the crime rate still remain.

I told the people that I was worried about the crime in the townships and unhappy that so many children were not attending school. I urged them to return to their classrooms.

I ended by opening my arms to all South Africans of goodwill, saying, "No man or woman who has abandoned apartheid will be excluded from our movement towards a non-racial, united and democratic South Africa."

*   *   *

That night, I returned with Winnie to number 8115, Orlando West. It was only then that I knew in my heart that I had really left prison.

When I saw our house, I was surprised at how small it was. It was the same size as the servant's quarters at the back of my cottage at Victor Verster.

I was happy to be home. I longed to return to a normal life and do the things that I had once done — like going to the office in the day and returning to my family at night, going shopping and visiting old friends. These are the things that I missed most in prison and dreamed about doing when I was free.

But I quickly began to realise that it was not going to be possible to lead a normal life. Every day for the next few weeks, the house was surrounded by well-wishers.

I could not turn them away. But in giving myself to my people, I could see that, once again, my family would be the ones who would suffer.

* * *

One of my first tasks after my release from prison was to report to the leadership of the ANC. On 27 February, I flew to Lusaka for a meeting with the National Executive Committee. It was wonderful to be reunited with comrades whom I had not seen for so many years.

While my comrades were pleased that I had been released, I could see that many of them had questions. Was this the same Mandela that they once knew? Had he become soft in prison? Had he survived his time in prison, or had he been broken? What had he agreed to with the South African government?

I explained what I had discussed with the government, clearly and carefully. I told them what demands I had made and what progress had been made.

At that NEC meeting, I was elected Deputy President of the organisation. Alfred Nzo was elected acting President, until Oliver recovered from his illness.

* * *

In the first six months after my release, I spent more time travelling to other countries than I spent at home.

I visited many countries in Africa. Later, I travelled to Europe and the United States. Wherever I went, I was met by huge and excited crowds.

I also flew to Stockholm to see my old friend and comrade, Oliver Tambo. I had not seen him for nearly 30 years.

With Oliver Jambo in Stockholm in 1990. Being with Oliver again after nearly 30 years was one of the happiest moments of my life.

Being with Oliver again was one of the happiest moments in my life. We were like two young boys again, taking strength from our love for each other.

❋ ❋ ❋

In March 1991, the ANC and the government planned to meet to discuss "talks about talks". But the meeting did not take place.

On 26 March, the police shot dead 12 ANC demonstrators, and wounded many more, in the township of Sebokeng. The police had used real bullets, and many of our people had been shot in the back as they were running away.

The ANC was furious and stopped talking with the government. We told Mr de Klerk that he could not talk about negotiations on the one hand, and murder our people on the other.

But even though the ANC had suspended the talks, I met Mr de Klerk privately, with the ANC's permission. We agreed on a new date for a meeting between our two organisations.

*　*　*

The first round of talks with the government was held over three days in early May. It took place at Groote Schuur, a large house that was once the home of Cecil Rhodes.

These first talks were conducted in a serious but friendly way. Thabo Mbeki said later that each side discovered that the other did not have horns. At the end of the three-day meeting, we agreed on what became known as the Groote Schuur Minute. Both sides agreed to a peaceful process of negotiations and an end to the State of Emergency. We also agreed to set up a joint working group to try to work out other problems that still stood in our way.

*　*　*

I wanted to go to Qunu immediately after my release from prison. But it was not until April 1991 that I was able to make the journey back to the place where I had grown up.

The first thing I did in Qunu was to visit the place where my mother was buried. As I stood beside her simple grave, I felt a deep sadness. I regretted that I was not able to be with her when she died, and that I had not been able to look after her properly during her life-time.

As I looked around Qunu, I noticed that a lot had changed but much had stayed the same. When I was a youngster growing up in the village, the people had had little to do with the struggle. But now, even school children were singing songs about Oliver Tambo and MK.

The warmth and simplicity of the community was still there. But what upset me was that the people seemed poorer than ever. Most people still lived in huts with dirt floors, with no electricity and no running water.

I remembered it as a village that was clean, where the water was pure and the grass was green. Now, the village was dirty and not properly cared for. The place was littered with plastic bags. It seemed to me that the people had lost pride in their community.

* * *

In the middle of July, shortly before there was to be a meeting of the National Executive Committee, Joe Slovo came to me privately with an idea. He suggested that we suspend the armed struggle so that the negotiations could move forward.

After thinking about it, I agreed with Joe, and we took the suggestion to the NEC. There was a long debate, but in the end they agreed.

On 6 August, the ANC and the government signed the Pretoria Minute. This was an agreement to suspend the armed struggle. As I was to say time and time again, we had suspended the armed struggle, but we had not ended it. We could go back to the armed struggle if necessary.

In December 1990, Oliver Tambo returned to South Africa, after almost 30 years in exile. He came back for the ANC's consultative conference in Johannesburg.

I paid tribute to Oliver at the conference. He was the man who had led the ANC during its darkest hours. He had built the organisation into a powerful force.

* * *

There were still many problems to solve before there could be a settlement in the country. The biggest problem was the violence in Natal and in the townships around Johannesburg. Much of this violence was between the ANC and Inkatha, led by Chief Buthelezi.

The violence upset me deeply and I arranged a meeting with Chief Buthelezi. In January, we met at a hotel in Durban and signed an agreement to end the violence.

But the violence continued between our organisations. I met Chief Buthelezi again in April and we signed another agreement. But before the ink was even dry, the blood was flowing again.

I began to believe, more and more, that the government was behind the violence. I felt that Mr de Klerk was not doing enough to stop it.

In April, the NEC called for the dismissal of Magnus Malan, the Minister of Defence, and Adriaan Vlok, the Minister of Law and Order. We also called for the carrying of traditional weapons in public to be banned, and for migrant-worker hostels in the townships to be closed down.

We gave the government until May to meet our demands. The government did nothing, and so we put a stop to the talks again.

* * *

In July 1991, the ANC held its first annual conference in South Africa in 30 years. I was elected as President of the ANC at that conference. Cyril Ramaphosa, who had been the leader of the National Union of Mineworkers, was elected as Secretary General.

At the conference I said that the government did not have the strength to continue with apartheid. This was why they wanted to negotiate. It was a victory for us.

I said that the struggle was not yet over. There was still a lot of work to do. But it was our duty to bring apartheid to an end as soon as possible. For this reason, negotiations could not wait.

* * *

On 20 December 1991, after more than a year and a half of talks about talks, the real talks began. The first real negotiations between the government, the ANC and other South African groups became known as CODESA — the Convention for a Democratic South Africa.

Eighteen delegations came together at the World Trade Centre in Kempton Park. It was the biggest gathering of leaders from different political organisations ever to meet in one place in South Africa.

The Pan-Africanist Congress and Inkatha boycotted the talks. But this did not dampen the sense of history that we all felt. We had taken our future into our own hands and, as fellow South Africans, we were settling our differences amongst ourselves.

* * *

At a press conference in Johannesburg on 13 April 1992, I announced that Winnie and I were to separate.

In my statement I said that we had been unable to have a normal family life because of our commitment to the ANC and the struggle.

I spoke of how she had supported and comforted me while I was in prison. I spoke of the courage she had shown in raising our children on her own. She had suffered much at the hands of the government, but her commitment to the freedom struggle had never wavered. I said that my love for her was still as strong as ever.

I went on to say that in recent months, tension had arisen between us. We both felt that it was best to separate.

I ended by saying, "I part from my wife with no recriminations. I embrace her with all the love and affection I have nursed for her inside and outside prison from the moment I first met her."

* * *

CODESA 2 started on 15 May 1992, after a four-month break. On the first day, the parties could not agree, but I was determined that the negotiations should continue.

The ANC and the Nationalist Party agreed that the two parties should continue to talk with each other. We had to find a way around our disagreements.

At the same time, as a way of putting pressure on the government, the ANC and its allies agreed on a policy of "rolling mass action".

The mass action, which was to start on June 16, 1992, consisted of strikes, demonstrations and boycotts. It was to end with a two-day national strike on 3 and 4 August.

But before we began, something else happened which drove the government and the ANC even further apart. On the night of 17 June 1992, a group of Inkatha members raided the Vaal township of Boipatong and killed 46 people. Most of the dead were women and children. It was the fourth mass killing of ANC people that week.

The police did nothing to stop the criminals. They did nothing to find them. Mr de Klerk said nothing. This was the last straw for me and I lost my patience. The government was making the negotiations difficult, and it was waging a secret war against our people.

Four days after the murders, I addressed a crowd of 20 000 angry ANC supporters. I told them that I had instructed Cyril Ramaphosa to stop talking to the government.

At this time, there were many people in the ANC who thought we should go back to the armed struggle. At first I agreed with this. But I soon realised that there was no choice but to continue with the negotiations. It was what I had been working towards for so many years and I would not turn my back on it now.

The mass action campaign was very successful. It ended with a general strike in which more than four million workers stayed at home. A hundred thousand people marched on the Union Buildings in Pretoria. I told the crowd that we would occupy these buildings one day as the first democratic government in South Africa.

*   *   *

On the morning of 7 September 1992, 70 000 protesters marched on the stadium in Bisho in the Ciskei. The troops of Brigadier Oupa Gqozo opened fire on the marchers, killing 29 people.

Like the old proverb that says that the darkest hour is before dawn, the tragedy at Bisho led to new negotiations.

Mr de Klerk and I met to try to find agreement. We both wanted to avoid another incident like the one at Bisho. We signed the Record of Understanding which created an independent group to look at police behaviour, to look into ways of fencing in the hostels, and to ban the carrying of traditional weapons at rallies.

And importantly, the Record of Understanding broke the deadlock in negotiations. The government finally agreed to accept a single, elected constitutional assembly which would write a new constitution and serve as a transitional government.

Inkatha were totally against the agreement. They announced their withdrawal from all further negotiations.

*   *   *

Once again, it was Joe Slovo who had a plan to help the negotiations to move forward. He proposed a government of national unity in which the ANC and the National Party, as well as other parties, would share power for a fixed length of time.

He suggested giving amnesty to people in the security forces. He also proposed that we give a promise to those in the civil service that they would not lose their jobs and pensions.

After much discussion, I supported the proposal, and it was also approved by the NEC.

In February, we announced to the country that we had agreed on a five-year government of national unity. After five years there would be a simple majority-rule government. The country would be governed by a transitional executive council until the election took place.

* * *

On 10 April, I was at my house in the Transkei on a brief holiday, when my housekeeper called me to the phone urgently.

I was told that Chris Hani had been shot dead in front of his home in Boksburg. He was the Secretary General of the Communist Party and one of the most popular leaders in the ANC.

Chris's death was a great blow to the ANC and to the country as a whole. He was one of South Africa's greatest sons, a man who could have made a big contribution to the building of a new nation.

His killers thought that they could stop the change to a democratic South Africa. But they did not succeed. Soon after Chris's death, I met with Mr de Klerk. We agreed that we would not let Chris Hani's murder upset the negotiations.

* * *

Exactly two weeks later, we suffered another great loss. Adelaide Tambo phoned me to say that Oliver had suffered another stroke. I rushed to his bedside, but I was too late. I did not have the chance to say a proper goodbye, for he was already gone.

Oliver's death shook me deeply. Though we had been apart for all those years that I was in prison, he was never far from my thoughts. I respected him greatly as a leader, and I loved him as a man.

We were not yet in power, but I wanted Oliver to have a state funeral, and that is what the ANC gave him. MK troops marched in his honour and a 21-gun salute was given at his graveside.

Oliver had lived to see the political prisoners released and the exiles returning home. But he had not lived long enough to cast his vote in a democratic South Africa. That bridge still had to be crossed.

*   *   *

Although few people will remember 3 June 1993, it was a historic day for South Africa. On that day, after months of negotiations, a date was set for the country's first democratic elections. These would take place on 27 April 1994.

Voters would elect 400 representatives to a constituent assembly. The assembly would write a new constitution and serve as a parliament.

Just after midnight on 18 November there was agreement on an interim constitution. This would be the law of the land until a final constitution was written. We were on the brink of a new era.

*   *   *

I have never cared very much for personal prizes. A person does not become a freedom fighter in the hope of winning awards. But I was deeply moved when I was told that I had won the 1993 Nobel Peace Prize jointly with F W de Klerk.

The award was a tribute to all South Africans, especially to those who had fought and died in the struggle for freedom. I would accept it on their behalf.

*   *   *

The ANC began campaigning for the coming elections as soon as the interim constitution was adopted.

In the first stage of the campaign, ANC leaders travelled

to all corners of the country, listening to people's hopes and fears, their ideas and complaints. We called these meetings People's Forums.

After getting suggestions from the people, we wrote our manifesto and travelled the country delivering our message. The slogan of our campaign was "A better life for all".

During the campaign, I reminded the people as often as I could that they should not expect miracles after the election. "Do not expect to be driving a Mercedes or have a swimming pool in your back yard," I said.

I told them that there was much work to be done. "If you want to continue living in poverty without clothes and food, then go and drink in the shebeens. But if you want better things, you must work hard. We cannot do it all for you; you must do it yourselves."

Many of our people cannot read and write, and so at every election meeting we taught people how to vote. "On election day," I said, "look down your ballot paper and when you see the face of a young and handsome man, mark an X."

* * *

The period before the election was not smooth. At first, Inkatha, the Conservative Party, the Afrikaner Volksfront and the Bophuthatswana government decided not to take part in the election.

I was very unhappy because I wanted as many people as possible to take part. We did our best to include everybody.

I was saddened by the violence that took place in the weeks leading up to the election. Many people died in battles between Mangope's troops and workers and students in Bophuthatswana, and between ANC and Inkatha members in Natal and in Johannesburg.

The people behind the violence did not want the election to take place. But Mr de Klerk and I stood firm. The election

147

would take place and nothing would make us change our minds.

I was very pleased when General Constand Viljoen brought his new party, the Freedom Front, into the elections. And I was delighted when, just a week before the election, Chief Buthelezi also agreed to take part.

* * *

It was a bright and clear day on 27 April 1994. On that day, millions of South Africans, from every corner of the country, made their way to the polling stations to cast their vote in the country's first ever democratic election.

The people stood patiently in long lines for their chance to vote for the party of their choice. There was a feeling of great joy in the air.

Old men and women who had never voted before said that they felt like human beings for the first time in their lives. Everybody, both black and white, spoke of their pride to be living in a free country at last.

I voted at a high school in Inanda, a green and hilly township just north of Durban. It is here that John Dube, the first President of the ANC, is buried.

As I stood over his grave, I did not think of the present, but of the past. I thought about all the men and women who had fallen in the struggle. I did not go into the voting station alone that day. I was casting my vote with all the people who had given their lives to make this day possible.

Before I entered the polling station, a journalist called out, "Mr Mandela, who are you voting for?"

"I have been thinking about that all morning," I answered.

I marked an X next to the letters "ANC" and then slipped the folded ballot paper into the wooden box. I had cast the first vote of my life.

* * *

27 April 1994: I slipped the ballot paper into the wooden box and cast the first vote of my life.

It took several days for the votes to be counted. The ANC won 62.6 per cent of the national vote, giving us 252 out of 400 seats in the National Assembly. We won big majorities in seven out of the nine provinces, losing only to Inkatha in KwaZulu/Natal, and to the National Party in the Western Cape.

* * *

On 10 May 1994, thousands of people gathered at the Union Buildings in Pretoria, which for so long had been the seat of white power and control.

I was sworn in as the country's first democratically elected President on 10 May 1994.

But no more. Now the gardens were filled with all the colours of the rainbow nation. They had come to witness my swearing-in as the country's first democratically elected President.

Mr de Klerk was sworn in as Second Deputy President, and Thabo Mbeki as First Deputy President. When it was my turn, I promised to uphold the constitution and to devote myself to the well-being of the country and its people.

I then addressed the gathering. I said that I believed that from the disaster of the past, a new society would be born which the world would be proud of. I spoke of how our victory belonged to everyone, for it was a victory for justice, for peace and for human dignity.

I said that we had at last won our political freedom, but that there was still work to be done. We still needed to free our people from poverty, suffering and all forms of discrimination.

I ended with the following words:

> Never, never and never again shall it be that this beautiful land will again experience the oppression of one by another ... the sun shall never set on so glorious a human achievement. Let freedom reign. God bless Africa!